STUDIES IN HISTORY, ECONOMICS AND PUBLIC LAW

EDITED BY THE FACULTY OF POLITICAL SCIENCE OF
COLUMBIA UNIVERSITY

Volume XXIII] [Number 2

MISTAKE IN CONTRACT

A STUDY IN COMPARATIVE JURISPRUDENCE

BY

EDWIN C. McKEAG, LL.B., Ph.D.

Sometime University Fellow in Columbia University

THE LAWBOOK EXCHANGE, LTD.

Clark, New Jersey

2003

ISBN-13: 978-1-58477-276-7
ISBN-10: 1-58477-276-X

Third printing 2007

THE LAWBOOK EXCHANGE, LTD.
33 Terminal Avenue
Clark, New Jersey 07066-1321

Please see our website for a selection of our other publications and fine facsimile reprints of classic works of legal history:
www.lawbookexchange.com

Library of Congress Cataloging-in-Publication Data

McKeag, Edwin Corwin.
Mistake in contract : a study in comparative jurisprudence / by Edwin C. McKeag.
p. cm.
Originally published: New York: Columbia University Press, 1905. (Studies in history, economics, and public law; v. 23, no. 2).
Includes bibliographical references.
ISBN 1-58477-276-X (cloth : alk. paper)
1. Contracts. 2. Mistake (Law) I. Title. II. Studies in history, economics, and public law; v. 23, no. 2

K860 .M35 2002
346.02—dc21 2002072856

Printed in the United States of America on acid-free paper

STUDIES IN HISTORY, ECONOMICS AND PUBLIC LAW

EDITED BY THE FACULTY OF POLITICAL SCIENCE OF
COLUMBIA UNIVERSITY

Volume XXIII] [Number 2

MISTAKE IN CONTRACT

A STUDY IN COMPARATIVE JURISPRUDENCE

BY

EDWIN C. McKEAG, LL.B., Ph.D.

Sometime University Fellow in Columbia University

New York

THE COLUMBIA UNIVERSITY PRESS

THE MACMILLAN COMPANY, AGENTS

LONDON: P. S. KING & SON

1905

PREFACE

THE discovery of the *echt* and *unecht* classes of mistake, however inappropriate these designations may be, has been said by Windscheid to have been one of the finest services which Savigny has rendered to jurisprudence. The former term comprises all those cases of contract in which consent exists, and which, though impeachable because of mistake, are valid until impeached. The latter term comprises those cases in which real consent is lacking, resulting in the nullity of the contract, while the mistake is simply an accompanying feature.

It has been the object of this dissertation to examine the latter, or *unecht*, class of mistake in the Roman law, to show the present development of the theory in modern civil law, mainly in Germany, and then to present some original treatment of the same subject in the common law. To the writer the latter theme has proved very interesting, for outside of the adjudicated cases there is no material, except in the writings of Pollock and Leake, who have treated the subject only as ancillary to the general law of contract. Proof, it is submitted, is given that the *unecht* class of mistake is unquestionably recognized in the common law, although a further important distinction has been made between mistake as to the act and mistake as to the content of the act, which distinction has not received general recognition in Germany. The paper will at least be an attempt to make a beginning in a field little cultivated heretofore by the writers on the common law.

Gratitude must be expressed to Professor Munroe Smith, under whom the writer pursued his work, not only for the use of some volumes not to be found in the Columbia Library, but especially for suggestions as to the proper scope and limitations of the paper as a dissertation and for criticism in the matter of style. E. C. McK.

NEW BRUNSWICK, NEW JERSEY, APRIL, 1905.

CONTENTS

INTRODUCTION

Nature of the Subject

PART I

ROMAN LAW

PART II

MODERN EUROPEAN LAW

CHAPTER I

Criticism of Savigny's Theory

PAGE

CHAPTER II

Modern Theories of Mistake

CHAPTER III

Negligence and Excusability

CHAPTER IV

Essentiality of Mistake

CHAPTER V

Error in Substantia

PAGE

CHAPTER VI

Nullity or Voidability

CHAPTER VII

Jhering's Negative Interest in Contracts

PART III

ANGLO-AMERICAN LAW

CHAPTER I

The Limitations of the Subject

CHAPTER II

Theories and Opinions

PAGE

CHAPTER III

Mistake as to the Act

CHAPTER IV

Mistake as to the Content of the Act

CHAPTER V

Mistake as to Fundamental Quality

CONCLUSION

INTRODUCTION

Nature of the Subject

Mistake, for the purpose of characterization in this article rather than by way of definition, may be said to consist simply in a lack of real consent. If I make a gift, but through aphasia, or some similar mental disturbance, designate and even deliver an object which I did not in fact have in mind, my consent is lacking. A person who marries the wrong party, as frequently happens when *schatchens* intermediate, has not really consented to such marriage. If I send an order for goods to one who has already sold out to his successor, and such successor fills out the order and sends me the bill, my consent is lacking, in the absence of knowledge on my part, to any liability to such successor. If I sign a deed thinking it to be a lease, my consent is absent. It is also absent when I sign any instrument whose content or purport is different from what I believed it to be. If I sell a piece of land according to a map, and sign a deed including more land than the map calls for, in the belief that the deed corresponds with the map, my consent is lacking to the transfer of the additional plot of land. Likewise a mortgagee does not give his consent to a loan upon the security of a term of years if the security is in fact a mere contingency in remainder. If I throw away a gold ring believing it to be brass, my consent to the abandonment or dereliction of the gold ring is absent. If some one pulls my door-bell and asks for some old newspapers, and I, upon glancing around, tell him to take a certain barrelful, forgetting that before leaving upon my vacation I had placed all of my silverware in the bottom of the barrel, in order to mislead possible thieves, my consent is lacking to the transfer of the silver. It is likewise lacking whenever I purchase any article believing that it possessed qualities and attributes which it did not in fact possess, and which, according to commonly accepted notions, would place the article in a category different from the one in which it must actually be placed.

All of these cases present instances of mistake involving an absence of true will, or a lack of real consent. The act or declaration or its content in each case is not intended or willed by the party subject to the mistake. The mistake accompanies and conceals a variation between the act or declaration and the will which should accompany it.

Mistake is a psychological concept, but a discussion of its psychological basis can be of very little assistance in the law. If a certain act or declaration is not intended or willed, if the consent to it is entirely lacking, the psychological and philosophical deduction is that there is no valid act or declaration. If the law were to start with this deduction, the entire subject of mistake would be extremely simple, for whenever this condition is present, nullity would necessarily be the only decree.

Upon general principles it is a fair conclusion that no one should be held liable for what he did not intend. In criminal law the intent is the essence of the act. In private law the intent is just as important. That such is the case is shown by the treatment accorded to the acts and declarations of lunatics, feeble-minded persons, drunkards when in a helpless condition, and persons known to be subject to certain mental diseases. In normal persons, also, the intent is an essential element. So far as the person is concerned who is laboring under the mistake, it is natural to assume the nullity of all acts and declarations to which the real consent of such person is lacking. The real difficulty is caused by the equities of the other party who is not laboring under any mistake, and who believes the particular act or declaration in question to be founded upon a corresponding will. It is manifestly unfair that such a party should suffer for the mistakes of another, or have his equities injuriously affected by mistakes of which he had not, and under the circumstances of the case could not be expected to have, any knowledge. In several of the above cases the only possible interests which could be affected are those of the party making the mistake. In all such cases there could be no hesitation in holding the act or declaration absolutely null. In others there is decided room for a difference of opinion, owing to the existence of equities which call loudly for protection.

The logical tendency, on the one hand, to hold that nullity must always follow when the real consent is absent, and the practical tendency, on the other hand, to protect the equities of innocent parties although the real consent of the mistaken party is absent, has led to the maintenance of two extreme doctrines of mistake or, more accurately, two theories of the juristic act.[1] The former may well be called the subjective theory, while the latter may be called the objective theory. Those who hold the former would insist in all events that if, in connection with a mistake, there is an essential variation between the will and expression, and a consequent lack of real consent to the act or declara-

[1] The phrase "juristic act" is a comparatively recent accession to English jurisprudence. It is the best possible translation of the German term "*Rechtsgeschäft*," long employed in German law to express the generic idea of an intentional legal act with definite consequences. In English law, the corresponding idea has always been expressed by the specific term in each instance. See Holland, *Jurisprudence*, p. 110.

tion in question, nullity must always follow, irrespective of all equities. Those who hold the latter theory would always insist that even though such a mistake should exist, with a consequent lack of real consent, yet validity must be decreed, because the sole criterion as to what the will is, is the act or expression itself.

Both of these views in their extremes are incorrect. Either, if applied inconsiderately, would be far from producing equitable results. Probably a mean between the two would represent the correct theory. The following is submitted: Whenever there is an unintentional variation between the will and its expression, with a consequent lack of real consent, nullity is to be decreed, unless there are manifest equities which, for their protection, require that a preponderating influence shall be given to the expression. The real problem, therefore, which presents itself is an investigation of the nature of these equities, together with the conditions under which, and the extent to which, they shall be protected. This is the task of the present article.

The treatment of the subject will be comparative. The theory of the Roman law as formulated by Savigny will be first stated as a basis. In connection with it, mistake in motive will have to be defined and treated in so far as may be necessary to differentiate the subjects and to secure clearness of argument in the succeeding sections. The next task will be to state the theories of later continental jurists, to discover the present continental doctrine of nullity on the ground of mistake, and to give the reasons for it. The final task will be the treatment of the common law upon the same subject and along the same lines.

PART I

ROMAN LAW[1]

THE existence in the Digest of Justinian of several passages to the effect that a mistake must always exclude the existence of the will, has led to the formulation of the apparently very simple doctrine that all juristic acts based on or induced by mistake are void.[2] The obstacle to the acceptation of this rule as final was found in the very clear doctrine of fraud (*dolus*). The doctrine of fraud assumed the validity of the contract until successfully attacked, either through the *actio doli* or through an *exceptio doli* to the action brought for the enforcement of the contract. The doctrine of mistake as interpreted from the passages in question assumed the nullity of the contract *ab initio*. The attempt to reconcile the two doctrines under a uniform theory of mistake led to infinite refinements and subtleties, the sole object of which was to conform the theory to the dicta and decisions in the Digest.

Savigny made a close study of the doctrine of fraud, and came to the conclusion that if a mistake were in itself sufficient to exclude the existence of the will or consent in one case, then it must have a similar effect in all cases.[3] The

[1] The authority upon this branch of the subject is Savigny, *System des heutigen römischen Rechts*, vol. iii.

[2] Dig. 2, 1, 15; 5, 1, 2, *pr.*; 39, 3, 20; and 50, 17, 116, § 2.

[3] Savigny, *System*, iii, p. 342.

principle in its nature could admit of no exception. It would, therefore, follow that a contract entered into through a mistake must be void at the beginning. Nothing, however, was more clear in Roman law than that a contract induced by fraud was *prima facie* valid. As a general rule, it could be attacked only through the *exceptio doli*, as a defense to the main action. Even in those rare cases in which the *actio doli* itself was permitted, *i. e.*, when there was no other legal remedy—a limitation due to the odious nature of the action, on account of the *infamia* attached to it—the contract itself was not considered as null. In fact, the *actio doli* was directed against the fraud rather than against the validity of the contract. Savigny, therefore, laid down the principle that in itself a mistake had absolutely no effect upon the production or failure of production of the juristic act, and that it could only in exceptional cases have any effect upon the operation of the juristic act after it was produced.

Savigny was also led to this conclusion by an analysis of the juristic act. He reasoned that all expressions and acts are merely attempts to make clear to others what the will actually is. Inasmuch as the will is something indiscernible, acting inwardly, it needs *indicia*, whereby it can be known to others. These *indicia* whereby the will is disclosed are precisely the expression, be it in the form of words or acts.[1] The agreement between the will and its expression is not an accidental but a natural relation.[2] The mere failure, therefore, of correspondence between the will and expression is in itself sufficient, under certain conditions, to render null any given act. The failure of correspondence may be due to mistake, or something else, but whatever the cause may be, it is the failure of correspondence alone, independ-

[1] Savigny, *System*, iii, p. 258. [2] *Ibid.*, pp. 258, 356.

ently of such cause, which is the true ground of nullity. If, therefore, in cases of fraud, it is not the mistake but the fraud that makes the act voidable, and if, in cases of non-correspondence between the will and its expression, it is lack of correspondence, and not a possible accompanying mistake, that constitutes the true ground of nullity, the rule that a mistake in itself has no possible effect or operation is doubly justified.

Searching through the texts of the Roman law, Savigny found ample support for his theses. He showed by the actual decisions that the existence of a mistake was never a direct cause of nullity. He who has made a gift in compensation for supposed services, which in fact were never rendered, cannot recover back his money.[1] When two persons bargain, and a third party lends false weights to the vendor, who is innocent, the mistake does not affect the validity of the sale, but the contract must be completed by giving full weight. The mistake is a ground neither of nullity nor for further fulfilment, which latter depends on the terms of the contract itself. If, however, the contract is expressly made dependent upon the particular weights employed, the *actio doli* lies against the third party, which proves that the contract is not null for mistake.[2] Again, if a creditor agrees to an *acceptilatio*, or discharge without payment, procured through the fraud of his debtor, the *actio doli* is permitted.[3] If in this case the discharge were void by reason of the creditor's mistake, he would have his original cause of action on the debt. If he had such a remedy, he would not be permitted to resort to the *actio doli*, which made the defeated defendant infamous. In this case,

[1] Dig. 12, 6, 65, § 2.

[2] Dig. 4, 3, 18, § 3.

[3] Dig. 4, 3, 38.

therefore, the proof is complete that the mistake does not affect the validity of the contract of release.

Were it not for such a rule as this, we should, in Savigny's opinion, be subjected in our daily business affairs to an intolerable degree of insecurity.[1]

To the rule that where consent exists mistake has regularly no significance, Savigny recognizes the following exceptions: First, the legal result which ordinarily attaches to an act or an omission may be expressly excluded by the law when the person acts or fails to act without knowledge of essential facts. Here the mistake operates directly; it excludes the ordinary legal result. Secondly, mistake may indirectly affect the legal results of an act, because the law gives a special but ordinary remedy, either in the form of an action or an exception. Thirdly, mistake may enable the person affected to apply for the extraordinary and equitable relief of *restitutio in integrum*.

Under the first exception may be mentioned the case of marriage with a widow during her period of mourning. If the marriage was entered into with knowledge of this fact, *infamia* was the penalty. Yet if it was an innocent act, the mistake operates directly to ward off the *infamia*.[2] Likewise an action to recover a loan made to a *filius familias* may be defeated through an *exceptio* raised under the *Senatus consultum Macedonianum*. Yet if the loan were made in ignorance of the fact that the defendant was a *filius familias*, the mistake operates directly to render the *exceptio* unavailable.[3]

The second exception includes all the cases of ordinary or regular relief from the legal results of an act because

[1] Savigny, *System*, iii, p. 355.

[2] Dig. 3, 2, 1; 3, 2, 8; and 3, 2, 11, § 4.

[3] Dig. 14, 6, 3.

of mistake. If one, through mistake, pays money which is not owed, the *condictio* was allowed for the purpose of recovering it.[1] This was the *condictio indebiti*, and was by far the most important of all the *condictiones sine causa*, or actions based on unjust enrichment. Again, when one buys an article which has a hidden defect, his mistake is sufficient ground for holding that he may either repudiate the purchase, or require a reduction in price. This he was enabled to do under the edict of the aediles.[2]

The third exception includes all cases of *restitutio* on account of mistake. *Restitutio* is an extraordinary remedy given in cases of damage resulting from innocent acts or omissions, and in favor of certain classes of persons. Such relief was granted with especial frequency in the case of acts and omissions in procedure. Thus, if a ward were sued in a case where a *falsus tutor* had given his *auctoritas*, a non-suit would follow for want of any ground of action, and legally no further action would lie. Yet if the ward had become enriched unjustly, a *restitutio* was granted by the praetor.[3] If a co-heir claimed to be the only heir, and a suit was brought against him for a debt due from the inheritance, the right of action was thereby lost as against the other co-heirs. But if the defendant was insolvent, the right of action was restored as against the others.[4] Whoever sued for more than he had a right to, lost all by *plus petendo*. But he could have his right of action restored provided he could show a justifiable mistake.[5] If a slave were accepted through mistake as bail or surety, the mistake was a ground of restitution or renewal of the secur-

[1] Dig. 12, 6, 1, § 1; and 12, 6, 7.
[2] Dig. 21, 1.
[3] Dig. 27, 6, 1, § 6.
[4] Dig. 11, 1, 18.
[5] Gaius, iv, § 53.

ity.[1] A confession in open court was binding, but if the confession was based upon a mistake, the party would be put in his former position prior to the mistake.[2] A mistake by a minor in loaning to a *filius familias*, or in accepting insufficient security, or in neglecting the period of *bonorum possessio*, will justify a *restitutio*.

It will be seen that in none of the above cases is the act void by reason of the mistake. There is no lack of correspondence between the will and its manifestation, and therefore the act is *per se* valid. The mistake operates only to affect the legal results of the act. The doctrine is, therefore, well justified that where there is real consent, mistake is in itself immaterial, save in exceptional instances. When mistake does operate by way of exception to the general rule, there are in each instance equities which, rather than the mistake alone, seem to be the real ground of relief. In other words, the remedy depends upon equitable features coupled with mistake. This view is borne out by Savigny when he maintains that each case must be considered by itself; that negligence regularly precludes all hope of relief; that there is a presumption of negligence in the case of mistake in law, but that it must be proved in the case of mistake in fact.

If we recur to the proposition, *nulla voluntas errantis est*, and consider in connection with it the cases above indicated, in which by way of exception an effect is attributed to mistake, we have an additional ground for repudiating the doctrine that mistake necessarily excludes consent, or is evidence of its absence. Most assuredly if such a doctrine were true, there would be no need whatever for the exceptions enumerated.[3] It would, therefore, seem that in

[1] Dig. 2, 8, 8, § 2.

[2] Dig. 11, 1, 13, *pr*.

[3] Savigny, *System*, iii, p. 356.

the light of every possible investigation, not only in the abstract, but also as supported by the actual decisions, the doctrine of mistake cannot be founded upon the general passages first above noted, which hold that a mistake necessarily excludes consent.

What, then, is the legitimate interpretation of such passages? Since the apparent meaning is evidently incorrect, they require special interpretation. They cannot be treated as independent passages. They require a study of the context and of related passages. Some of the cases in which the phrase is used are as follows: When an owner, through mistake, believes that his property belongs to another, and verbally expresses such an opinion, his ownership is not at all affected.[1] Neither is it affected when, through mistake as to the ownership, he agrees to assist a stranger in a real action for its recovery.[2] The same must be held when, through such a mistake, he permits a stranger to enjoy the fruits.[3] The basis of such decisions as these, as Savigny points out, is that the nullity depends not on the mistake, but on the absence of any binding legality in the acts in question. The passages in question, therefore, cannot be taken in a literal sense. They merely mean that, under the particular conditions of the given case, the transaction in question, presenting itself under the aspect of mistake, is null and void.[4]

The true doctrine of the Roman law is that a mistake has absolutely no effect in preventing the formation of a legal relationship, and only a limited effect in exceptional cases in excluding or modifying the legal results which ordinarily attach to such a relationship; and that even in these exceptional cases mistake cannot be pleaded if the

[1] Cod. 3, 32, 18.
[2] Dig. 6, 1, 54.
[3] Dig. 31, 79.
[4] Savigny, *System*, iii, p. 343.

party was guilty of culpable negligence. But limited as these exceptional cases are, we must recognize the fact that in them, and in them alone, is the mistake the ground of relief. They are the only cases in which we can speak of mistake as affecting legal relations.

We cannot speak of the effects of a mistake except in those cases in which the usual and regular results of such juristic acts as depend upon the free will are excluded or modified through the existence of a mistake, because in view of such mistake the will is regarded as incomplete.[1]

It is in such cases that Savigny calls the mistake *echt*, or genuine, because of its direct effect or influence upon the juristic act. Other cases of mistake, he insists, are not genuine or real, because it is not the mistake that is really significant, or that affects the juristic act.

If the case in which a mistake occurs is in itself so constituted that it lacks the necessary conditions of a juristic fact, it is not the mistake which excludes the consequences of such a fact, and it is therefore incorrect to speak of any operation of the mistake in these cases. . . . Such cases may be designated as *unechter Irrthum.*[2]

The second category is of very great importance. In this class of mistakes it is the unintentional variation between will and expression which is the ground of nullity. Mistake is always present, and is undoubtedly the cause of the variation between the will and its expression; but the utmost that can be said for it is that it is an indirect cause of the nullity of the juristic act. Savigny, however, ignores even this indirect operation of the mistake and insists that

[1] Savigny, *System*, iii, p. 440.

[2] *Ibid.*

it is the variation alone which causes the nullity. "The mistake," he says, "is of importance in so far as we can recognize from it the fact that the will, which, in view of the declaration would necessarily be assumed to exist, is in fact not present, for which reason the legal consequences of the will cannot ensue." [1]

In this class of cases it must be remembered that the variation between will and declaration is always unconscious. The two other forms of variation, *i. e.*, concealed or mental reservation, which is a species of fraud, and unconcealed intentional variation, which is best illustrated by the drama, are both conscious, and being for this reason entirely unconnected with the subject of mistake are excluded from consideration in the present discussion.

The unconscious variation between the will and its declaration does not exclude consent and make the act void unless the variation is important, or "essential." The customary list of essential mistakes includes the following classes: mistake as to the nature of the legal relationship; mistake as to the identity of the person; and mistake as to the identity of the object, including mistake *in substantia*.

In each of these classes we perceive a mistake accompanying the juristic act, and from this fact we can always recognize the absence of the true will and likewise a resulting invalid juristic act. But it is not every accompanying mistake which will warrant the assertion of such absence, and it is therefore of great importance that we should lay down precise limits within which an influence is to be attributed to a mistake. The authorities have united in holding that only an essential mistake shall be taken into consideration, while all those of a trivial nature shall be ignored in ascertaining the existence of the will.[2]

[1] *Ibid.*, iii, p. 264. [2] *Ibid.*, iii, pp. 267, 268.

Mistake as to the nature of the legal relationship occurs, for example, when one loans an article or sum of money to another, who understands the transaction as a gift. In this instance the binding obligation which is incident to a loan does not attach to the party making such a mistake.[1] The transaction is, therefore, neither a loan nor a gift, and the plaintiff must seek his remedy in a *vindicatio*, or real action, or in a *condictio* based on a quasi-contractual obligation. Likewise if one makes a present of money to one who thinks it is a loan, the relationship peculiar to a loan does not arise.[2] But in this latter case the transaction operates as a gift, because the mistaken party has no beneficial interest in asserting his lack of consent. The fact that one is mistaken as to what legal relationship he is entering into presents a case of essential mistake, and will, therefore, result in the nullity of the juristic act or contract. The only modification of this principle arises through the absence of a beneficial interest, which might otherwise be affected.

A mistake in the identity of the person exists, for example, when a testator names in writing a certain person as his heir, having beyond doubt a different person in view, whom he has confused with the person actually named. Such an appointment is void; but the unexpressed intent is also ineffective, and neither party can take.[3] The same is truc in the case of a nuncupative will, when the testator points out the person whom he intends for his heir or legatee, but through weakness of sight or the darkness of the room identifies the wrong person.[4] If a marriage is entered into by mistake with the wrong person, it is abso-

[1] Savigny, *System*, iii, p. 269.
[2] *Ibid.*, iii, p. 269.
[3] Dig. 28, 5, 9, *pr.*
[4] Savigny, *System*, iii, p. 270.

lutely void. If I intend to make a loan to a person whom I have never seen, and a different person is fraudulently imposed upon me, there is no valid loan to such a stranger, and the ownership of the money is not affected. Such a recipient, if he acted fraudulently, would be treated as a thief.[1] If I take a loan thinking it was from Gaius, when in fact it was from Seius, there is no valid obligation of the character of a loan.[2] Seius would have nothing but a quasi-contractual right of action against me. Seius gave the money as a loan, but such relationship was frustrated by the mistake as to the person.

It frequently happens, however, that the identity of the particular person is immaterial. So long as one sustains no detriment from the mistake and derives from the transaction the advantage which is the principal object, it is a matter of indifference whether the particular person thought of is brought into a legal relationship or not. This is commonly the case in sales of petty merchandise. The principle, however, is very clear that a mistake as to the identity of the person may be essential and competent to cause a nullity of the contract.

Finally, the mistake as to the identity of the object may be illustrated by the case of a testator bequeathing an object which he has confused with something else.[3] This is the common case of *error in corpore*. In the contract of sale, if the vendor and the vendee each intend a different object, there can be no valid contract. Likewise in the contract of hiring and letting, there must be an actual and not a merely apparent meeting of the minds as regards the object.[4] In the *donatio*, and also in the *stipulatio*, the parties must in reality, and not merely in appearance, both intend the same

[1] Dig. 47, 2, 52, § 21, and 47, 2, 67, § 4.
[2] Dig 12, 1, 32.
[3] Dig. 28, 5, 9, § 1, and 30, 4, *pr.*
[4] Dig. 18, 1, 9, *pr.*

thing.[1] Delivery (*traditio*) cannot take place without a clear perception of the object.[2] Otherwise delivery would not merely furnish a basis for usucapion but would give rise to ownership, when there is no such intention nor right founded upon knowledge.[3]

In one case only [Savigny says] will such a misunderstanding in regard to particular objects fail to impair the validity of juristic acts, *viz.*, in procedure. If, for example, at the end of a legal controversy the defendant asserts that he had in mind a different object from that which the plaintiff was suing for, no attention will be paid to his assertion, because the admission of such pleas would tend to frustrate the effective administration of justice.[4]

When the mistake is as to the kind, we have in reality a mistake *in corpore*. A mistake *in genere* is just as important as a mistake concerning a special thing (*in specie*). An apparent agreement to buy rye when wheat was intended is not binding.

If, however, the mistake is as to quantity, it is necessary to consider the question of *consensus* a little more carefully than in other instances. If one party is thinking of a larger amount than his opponent is contemplating, the contract may be void for the larger amount but valid for the smaller, because there may be *consensus* or a meeting of the minds at least with regard to the smaller if not the larger amount.[5] For example, if an owner of a house offers to lease the house to one who thought he said twenty dollars a month, when in fact he asked only ten, the contract is valid for ten dollars a month. On the other hand, if the lessee understood the rental to be five when the lessor was asking ten, there is no *consensus*, and consequently no contract.[6]

[1] Dig. 45, 1, 83, § 1, and 45, 1, 137, § 1.
[2] Dig. 41, 2, 34, *pr.*
[3] Dig. 41, 4, 2, § 6.
[4] Savigny, *System*, iii, pp. 273, 274.
[5] Dig. 45, 1, 1, § 4.
[6] Dig. 19, 2, 52.

We have now to consider the case of mistake in substance (*in substantia*). The Roman law, as a general rule, treated a mistake in quality as immaterial. There are, however, certain exceptional cases in which such a mistake is treated precisely like a mistake *in corpore*. As Savigny points out, it is quite necessary to keep such exceptions within sharply defined limits. Otherwise a mistake as to the characteristics of an object would exclude the will and result in nullity in such a great number of cases that all security in daily intercourse would be at an end.[1] It cannot be said, therefore, that nullity will follow in every case of a mistake as to a characteristic. The Roman law recognizes nullity in the following cases only: base metals are taken to be gold or silver; objects plated with gold or silver are taken to be solid; vinegar is supposed to be wine; or the mistake is as to the sex of a slave.[2] In each of these specific cases it is assumed that there is no *consensus*, and that the act of the purchaser is void. The treatment, therefore, is precisely as if the mistake were *in corpore*.

What, then, is the principle upon which any given mistake *in substantia* is to be regarded as essential, *i. e.*, as excluding the will and thereby producing a nullity of the juristic act or contract? It was long maintained that the question depended upon the intrinsic value of the article, as distinguished from its commercial value. Savigny saw that the criterion of value was not sufficient, because of the absence of definite limitations.[3] When shall we say that such intrinsic value exists? How far shall we go? These are questions which leave room for a difference of opinion. The criterion of value, moreover, whether intrinsic or com-

[1] Savigny, *System*, iii, p. 277.

[2] *Ibid.*, iii, p. 278. *Cf.* Dig. 18, 1, 9, § 2; 18, 1, 10; 18, 1, 11, § 1; 18, 1, 14; and 18, 1, 41, § 1.

[3] Savigny, *System*, iii, p. 279.

mercial, would not apply to the case of vinegar mistaken for wine; for even though the vinegar in question be of a special variety and much more costly than the wine intended, the lack of consent would make the sale void. A mistake as to the sex of a slave was also essential, independently of the question of value. The only safe rule requires the identification of the object in question with what it is supposed to be. Savigny, therefore, holds that a mistake as to a characteristic or property of an article is essential only when such article, according to the views commonly prevalent in daily intercourse, must be held to be practically different from what it was supposed to be.[1]

Adopting this rule, we can at once decide upon the essentiality of the characteristics in any given case. Thus a mistake as to paste diamonds is essential and results in a nullity of the sale, because the mistake in substance is, from a practical standpoint, equivalent to a mistake *in corpore*. Paste diamonds and real diamonds are different things. In the purchase of an animal, the question is whether, according to common opinion, it is so entirely different from what it was supposed to be that there is no identity. The rule is thus applicable almost indefinitely. Such a rule could be applied to the case of a sale of a house which was supposed at the time to be in existence, but had in fact been burned.[2] The sale is technically of the ground, which carries with it the house, but in our daily intercourse the site of a burned building is viewed as something different from a house and lot, and the contract would be void. Cases of this sort were decided by the Romans upon the theory of impossibility of performance, and their decisions have, strictly speaking, nothing to do with the subject of mistake. The analogy, however, is instructive.

On the other hand, we have examples of mistake in qual-

[1] Savigny, *System*, iii, p. 283.

[2] Dig. 18, 1, 57, *pr*.

ity which are not essential. Thus, a mistake as to the purity or fineness of gold is no ground of nullity.[1] The substance is still gold, however poor in quality. A mistake in buying inferior wine is not essential.[2] The purchase of an old slave supposed to be young is binding.[3] A mistake in buying old clothing supposed to be new is of no moment.[4] The same reasoning must be applied, according to Savigny, in regard to the purchase of furniture, the price of which varies greatly according to the kind of wood employed.[5] A mistake as to the kind of wood is a mistake in quality, but cannot be treated as a mistake *in corpore*. Such a sale is, therefore, not void, and relief is dependent upon the question whether or not the vendor made any representations.[6] No reasonable person would hold that a purchaser of a cherry table should be released from his bargain because he thought it was mahogany. Such a mistake in quality is without the rule, and cannot be called essential.

It is of peculiar interest that in all those cases of mistake in quality which were treated as essential, the Roman law never gave relief through any remedy which recognized the validity of the act until it was impeached. Of necessity we must infer that the Roman law regarded such acts as void rather than voidable. The treatment, therefore, is precisely similar to mistake *in corpore*. As Savigny puts it, the will is entirely excluded by an essential mistake in quality, and consequently the nullity of the juristic act or contract must follow.[7] This fact, he contended, was shown not only by a treatment analogous to that of mistake *in corpore*, but also by special passages.[8] Such a mistake belonged to Savigny's *unecht* class.[9]

[1] Dig. 18, 1, 10; 18, 1, 14.

[2] Dig. 18, 1, 9, § 2.

[3] Dig. 18, 1, 11, § 1; 19, 1, 11, § 5.

[4] Dig. 18, 1, 45.

[5] Dig. 19, 1, 21, § 2.

[6] Savigny, *System*, iii, p. 289.

[7] *Ibid.*, iii, p. 291.

[8] Dig. 18, 1, 9, § 2.

[9] Savigny, *System*, iii, p. 292.

PART II

MODERN EUROPEAN LAW

CHAPTER I

Criticism of Savigny's Theory

The selection of the term *unecht* by Savigny has led to some confusion. To one who has not read Savigny's writings, the natural inference would be that a mistake which is not genuine is one which is merely apparent and not real. Nothing, however, could have been further from Savigny's idea. His *unechter Irrthum* is no less real than his *echter*, and is by far the more important.

The best criticism of Savigny upon this point is that of Windscheid. "An *unechter Irrthum*," he says, "is a mistake which is only apparently a mistake, but not a mistake which only apparently exercises a certain legal result." [1] He would not, however, because of this mere inaptness of terms, discard the distinction itself as unjustifiable, as Bekker would do.[2] Windscheid holds that the distinction is epoch-making; and while it may have been improved upon by recent writers along the original lines, it is the only one which can serve as a foundation for a satisfactory theory

[1] Windscheid, *Pandekten*, i, sec. 76, n. 1.

[2] "Zur Civilistischen Literatur," *Kritische Vierteljahrsschrift*, iii, pp. 187, *et seq.*

of mistake, and its discovery is one of the finest services rendered by Savigny.[1]

Savigny's *echter Irrthum* is identified by Windscheid and many other writers with "mistake in motive" (*Irrthum im Beweggrund*[2])—an identification for which Savigny himself, in several passages, furnishes at least a suggestion. For the *unechter Irrthum*, Dernburg uses the phrase, "mistake in the act" (*Geschäftsirrthum*[3])—a phrase which is, perhaps, open to the objection that it may be confused with mistake as to the nature of the act (*error in negotio*). Pollock uses the term, "fundamental error."[4]

But aside from terminology, the analysis by Savigny of the function of his *unechter Irrthum* calls for remark. Savigny was correct in holding that it was not the mistake, but the failure in correspondence, which caused the nullity of the juristic act. Was he not wrong, however, in holding that a mistake is simply an auxiliary feature of the failure in correspondence? Is it not something more than this? Is it not the real cause of the failure in correspondence, and therefore indirectly of the nullity of the juristic act? These questions, it seems to the writer, must be answered in the affirmative. The mistake is the cause, the nullity is the result of the failure in correspondence. It must, therefore, follow that the mistake, while not a direct, is certainly an indirect cause of the nullity of the juristic act.[5] Savigny was probably induced to treat the mistake as a mere accompaniment, because of his appreciation of the cardinal principle that an act unsupported by the will is no valid act.

[1] Windscheid, *Pandekten*, i, sec. 76, n. 1. *Cf.* Zitelmann, *Irrtum und Rechtsgeschäft*, pp. 7, 8.

[2] Windscheid, *Pandekten*, i, sec. 76, n. 1. and sec. 78.

[3] Dernburg, *Pandekten*, i, sec. 101.

[4] Pollock, *Principles of Contract*, p. 412.

[5] Compare Zitelmann's negative function of mistake, *infra*, chap. ii.

A third criticism of greater importance arises in connection with the case of mental reservation. The ground of Savigny's decision in this class of cases rests on the right of a man to rely upon the "trustworthiness of those signs whereby alone men can carry on the affairs of life with one another." [1] For this reason, and because the variation is intentional, the juristic act is treated as if it were founded upon a real will. But the ground of decision is purely equitable, and equally applicable to the case of unintentional variation. The omission of this equitable principle from consideration, except in connection with cases of mental reservation, constitutes a defect in Savigny's theory. Its admission does not destroy the nullity theory, for its operation is entirely by way of exception, or as collateral relief on account of the damage flowing from the nullity of the juristic act. The equities of the person who has relied upon the declaration constitute a strong argument for the objective theory of contract. Leonhard quotes it on his side.[2] These equities, however, have been recognized and satisfied in the new German civil code, without abandonment of the subjective theory, by means of the doctrine of negative interest in contract.[3]

The fact that nullity follows as a result of Savigny's theory, notwithstanding the absolutely inexcusable nature of the mistake, has provoked a good deal of controversy. From the standpoint of justice it would seem that a mistake caused by gross negligence ought not to present a means of escape from the obligations of a contract. As will be shown later, this was the position assumed in the German draft code. In its final form, however, the German civil code pursues the opposite course, and in accordance with

[1] Savigny, *System*, iii, p. 258. [2] Leonhard, *Der Irrthum*, p. 6.

[3] See *infra*, chap. vii.

Savigny's views treats the juristic act or contract as invalid, entirely independently of the question whether or not the mistake be inexcusable. Relief from the apparent injustice and hardship is fully secured through the doctrine of negative interest just mentioned.

All the matters here touched upon call for more or less extended consideration. In the first place, however, a brief examination of the various theories of mistake as associated with the production of the juristic act will be useful. The two extremes of the subjective and objective theories cannot well be preserved; they tend to shade imperceptibly into each other. Very few writers have maintained the strict doctrine of Savigny in its entire detail. The best method, therefore, will be to treat the various theories with reference to Savigny's doctrine as a standard.

CHAPTER II

Modern Theories of Mistake

Leonhard, in his treatise on the subject of mistake as a ground of nullity, proposes to found his argument upon Savigny's theory. This theory, however, he interprets in a manner which is not only novel, but unjustifiable. He admits that the prevailing doctrine requires an agreement between the will and expression, but urges that this is a perversion of Savigny's theory, and that the adherents of such a view are wrongly called the partisans of Savigny. "It is certain," he says, "that the prevailing doctrine no longer really proceeds from the standpoint of Savigny, whose views have been so quickly forgotten that those who rely on the will as the criterion rather than upon the terms of the contract are regarded as his partisans." [1] According to Leonhard, the true interpretation of Savigny's theory is that the expressions must agree with the wills, but if the will of one of the parties is not correctly expressed, and this fact is not and cannot be known to the other party, then the expression is the controlling factor. He further hopes most heartily that after a short displacement, Savigny's view (as he regards it) will again resume its rightful position of honor.[2]

In order to substantiate this interpretation, it is necessary to show that Savigny treated the expression as the controlling factor in the case of the *unechter Irrthum*. Leonhard first cites Savigny's statement of the requisites of

[1] Leonhard, *Der Irrthum*, p. 8. [2] *Ibid.*, p. 7.

a contract, that the parties "must have willed something definitely, and must both have willed the same thing, for so long as there is either indecision or lack of agreement, no one will be able to assume the existence of a contract." [1] This statement, Leonhard thinks, might be interpreted either way, and he therefore goes on, without examining the context of the sentence just cited, to Savigny's definition of contract, on the following page. This definition reads: "Contract is the uniting of two or more persons in a harmonious declaration of wills, whereby the legal relation between them is determined." [2] In this sentence Leonhard finds evidence that the declaration and not the will is, in Savigny's opinion, the decisive element. It should be noted, however, that the word "*Willenserklärung*" embraces both elements and lays decisive emphasis on neither. It should further be noted that before taking up the special subject of contract, in the section from which the preceding sentences are extracted, Savigny declares that contract is but a special category of *Willenserklärungen*, although the most important and comprehensive category.[3] It is to the *Willenserklärung* in general that the preceding two hundred pages of Savigny's treatise are devoted, and in these he repeatedly insists on the essentiality of each of the two elements, will and declaration. Only where the variation between will and declaration is intentional and secret (mental reservation) does the declaration prevail absolutely over the will, and in approaching these cases he indicates their exceptional character by premising: "Really the will *per se* must be thought of as the only important and efficient thing; and it is only because it is an internal and invisible occurrence that we need a sign whereby it may be recognized by others." [4]

[1] Savigny, *System*, iii, p. 308.
[2] *Ibid.*, p. 309.
[3] *Ibid.*, p. 307.
[4] *Ibid.*, p. 258.

Leonhard goes back to this portion of Savigny's treatise only for the purpose of wresting a sentence from its context.

It appears as though Savigny had felt the necessity of avoiding any possible misunderstanding by means of an especially clear statement, for he [Savigny] remarks: "Accordingly a contradiction between the will and its expression can be assumed to exist only in so far as it is or becomes cognizable by the party who comes into immediate contact with the declarant." [1]

It appears, however, to have entirely escaped Leonhard's attention that the section from which this quotation is taken[2] deals wholly with intentional variations, and that the sentence immediately preceding deals with the mental reservation. In the following sections,[3] which treat of unintentional variations, there is nowhere any allusion to the recognition or non-recognition by the other party of the declarant's mistake, but repeated affirmations that the absence of intent in any essential point results in the nullity of the act.[4]

Aside from the attempt to drag Savigny into the matter, Leonhard's theory is worthy of consideration. He asserts that the doctrine of mistake can and should be expressed in

[1] Leonhard, *Der Irrthum*, p. 5, citing Savigny, *System*, iii, p. 259.

[2] Savigny, *System*, iii, sec. 134.

[3] *Ibid.*, secs. 135–139, pp. 257–307.

[4] In ascribing to Savigny the confession "that a difference between '*Wille*' and '*Willenserklärung*' is important only when it can be known to others," Holland (*Jurisprudence*, p. 114, n. 3) has evidently been misled by Leonhard. It seems that he has simply followed Leonhard, for he cites the same passage from Savigny which Leonhard cites, and gives the same page number which Leonhard gives, but without reference to succeeding pages. The passage in question appears in fact on the page of Savigny's treatise succeeding the page which Holland cites.

terms of implied conditions precedent. He states that mistakes of a contracting party can affect the validity of the contract only when they relate to circumstances, a correct conception of which is indicated to the other contracting party, in a discernible way, as an indispensable condition precedent to the validity of the contract.[1] If the parties are mistaken in regard to such circumstances, then the contract is null. According to his view, it is absolutely immaterial what the mistake is about. He abolishes all classification. His doctrine is directly applicable to any and all cases without distinction.[2] The question as to when the contract is null for mistake is dependent upon the significance which, according to the interpretation of the declarations, must be attributed to the point or circumstance in regard to which a mistake exists.[3] Do the parties regard the point or circumstance in such a light that its correctness is a condition precedent to the validity of the contract? If so, a mistake as to such point or circumstance is a ground of nullity. But if only one of the parties is mistaken, and such fact is not and cannot be known to the other party, then it cannot be said that the contract has been entered into mutually by both parties upon the assumption of the correctness of the particular point or circumstance. Hence, such correctness in this latter case is not a condition precedent to the validity of the contract.

Leonhard's doctrine may be best defined as a peculiar method of interpretation of the contractual declarations.[4] Assuming that the theory is correct, its adoption would require the formulation of new rules of evidence. How and when shall we admit the existence of such conditions precedent as those proposed by Leonhard? How can we

[1] Leonhard, *Der Irrthum*, p. 512.
[2] *Ibid.*, p. 398.
[3] *Ibid.*, pp. 280, 287.
[4] *Ibid.*, pp. 166–171.

safely identify them in practice? When are they so discernible that the other party is bound to discern them? Leonhard attempts to answer these questions by laying down the limitations as to tacit, presumed, express and fictitious declarations and their proper interpretation. But all this is merely opinion. These questions could be resolved into safe rules of evidence only after years of experience.

Leonhard's views, as he states them, suggest a compromise between the subjective and objective theories. His conception of the function of the will in contracts is that the will can be realized only in so far as it is actually expressed through the medium of a juristic act.[1] It is the juristic act and not the will as such to which the law gives effect. Nevertheless the act must be willed, otherwise no obligation can arise. Accompanying the juristic act based upon the will there may, however, be conditions precedent upon which the validity of the contract is to depend. In these propositions is contained, as he claims, the essence of his whole doctrine of mistake.[2]

In reality Leonhard's theory is objective; for an indicated condition is part of the declaration, and the acceptance by the other party of a declaration thus conditioned is treated as an acceptance of the condition. Whether the other party did or did not perceive the condition is of no consequence, if under the circumstances he ought to have perceived it. Nothing could be more objective than this.

It is perhaps worth noting that if Leonhard's theory be pushed to its logical consequences, such conditional contracts as he assumes can never fail by reason of mistake. According to his construction both parties are taken to have willed the same result under the same condition precedent. The only mistake on their part which he will recognize relates to

[1] Leonhard, *Der Irrthum*, p. 114.

[2] *Ibid.*, p. 115.

the existence of the circumstances on which the condition hinges. If their assumption in this respect proves incorrect, their contract fails, not by reason of their mistake nor against their wills, but because of the failure of the condition precedent and according to their wills. Thus Leonhard solves the problem of mistake in contract by eliminating mistake as a determinant factor.

As will be seen later,[1] implied conditions precedent are recognized in English judicial decisions; but no such extension has been given to the doctrine as is proposed by Leonhard.

Of all writers, excepting possibly Bähr and Röver, Hartmann [2] presents the most conclusive argument against the unqualified acceptance of the subjective theory. He approaches the question from the practical side. Suppose one goes to a druggist and calls by mistake for a different preparation from that which he intends to order. In such a case, Hartmann would draw a distinction. If the preparation called for is one usually kept on hand, it is fair to correct the mistake. If it has to be specially compounded, and if, before the mistake is perceived, the druggist has actually compounded it, the party who made the mistake should pay for it. To enforce the pure will theory in such cases as this would be to hold that "those having foresight must bear the damage, while the negligent, who acted through mistake, go free from its consequential damage." [3] Hartmann admits the force of the subjective theory, but insists that the needs of everyday life, from the practical point of view, require that some declarations which are not

[1] See *infra*, part iii, chap. i.

[2] "Wort und Wille in Rechtsverkehr," in *Jahrbücher für Dogmatik*, vol. xx, pp. 1–79.

[3] *Ibid.*, pp. 1–3.

willed be treated as valid.[1] The rule which he proposes is the rule of good faith:

The conscious author of the outward substance of a juristic act may be held responsible for such act, without regard to his subjective ideas and purposes, whenever *bona fides* and the necessary consideration for the security of daily intercourse forbid that the deviating inner will be taken into account. . . . In interpreting contracts, modern practice has turned its back entirely upon the inner movements of the will, whenever confidence and good faith in trade and commerce [*Handel und Wandel*] require it.[2]

The purely objective theory is represented by Bähr, for whom Hartmann expresses admiration.[3] Bähr [4] states the following case, decided by the *Oberamtsgericht* in Berlin. The defendant was sued for 600 thalers on a negotiable instrument, which he was induced by his debtor to sign in the belief that it was for 600 marks. His sight was defective, he did not have his glasses at hand, and he signed without close scrutiny. The court said that "it would undermine all security in commercial dealings and destroy all good faith if a declaration made in the most binding form, with the object of entering into a contract, could be set aside simply by proof that it was not in harmony with the real will." The court added that "a difference between the will and expression, which subsequently comes to light, must be taken into consideration by the other party in so far as this is required by the good faith which governs the common dealings of life." [5] This case, which is cited by Hartmann also,[6] is quite in accord with the latter's theory,

[1] *Ibid.*, pp. 10–13. [2] *Ibid.*, pp. 65, 66. [3] *Ibid.*, p. 68.

[4] "Ueber Irrungen im Contrahiren" in *Jahrbücher für Dogmatik*, xiv, pp. 393–427.

[5] *Ibid.*, xiv, p. 426. [6] *Ibid.*, xx, p. 63.

but the grounds on which the decision is based are not those on which Bähr insists. The well-known case of the telegram from a house in Cologne to one in Frankfort, in which the word "*kaufen*" was inserted by mistake of the operator in place of the word "*verkaufen*," calls forth the approval of Bähr. The court decided that the loss caused by the drop in quotations must be made good by the Cologne firm, thus upholding the pure objective theory of contract, independently of the question of good faith.[1]

The doctrine laid down by Bähr is substantially as follows: Whenever, in making a contract, one party is responsible for creating the impression of a serious intention, so that the other party honestly thinks and is justified in thinking that he has thereby acquired rights, the responsible party cannot be heard to say that in reality he had no such intention.[2]

Röver [3] draws a distinction between testamentary acts and all other acts. He upholds the will theory as to the former, because the authorities, as well as the "nature of the thing," requires it.[4] He, however, condemns it as regards all acts *inter vivos*, because it ignores the element of excusability, and is therefore productive of great injustice.[5] "The nature of the thing," he says, is against the results attained. Declarations between living persons are *per se* meant to be binding. Röver thinks the subjective theory is untenable, as regards acts *inter vivos*, for three reasons. First, one cannot say that it is in the majority of cases actually applied. Second, it leads to very inequitable consequences. Third, the nature of the thing is against it. He thinks that the cases in the Digest, which apparently sustain

[1] *Ibid.*, xiv, p. 393. [2] *Ibid.*, xiv, p. 401.

[3] *Ueber die Bedeutung des Willens bei Willenserklärungen* (Rostock, 1874).

[4] *Ibid.*, p. 3. [5] *Ibid.*, p. 9.

it, are all in reality cases of *dissensus, i. e.,* divergence of declarations, and not of divergence between the will and the declaration of one party.[1]

Regelsberger [2] admits that logically the will and expression must agree. He insists, however, that the demands and necessities of daily intercourse are directly opposed to the consequences of such a rule. These demands and necessities require that the declarant shall be held responsible for his words, although they are not the expression of his will. This statement is emphasized in the case of contracts.

> Every one who in contractual relations makes a declaration is liable according to that interpretation which the other party put upon it, or was bound to put upon it, according to all the circumstances which were known to him, or may be assumed to have been known to him, at the time when the contract was concluded. Apart from a mistake which does not appear to be due to gross negligence, no different intention [on the part of the declarant] will be considered even though such different intention may be made entirely clear from extraneous circumstances.[3]

Although he emphasizes the importance of the declaration, Regelsberger does not belong to the purely objective school, for he allows mistake to be pleaded even when the mistaken party was somewhat negligent.

Schlossman [4] holds that the declarant should be bound by his declaration, although it was not willed, if the variation was not known to the other party. He argues that when an express or tacit promise is made, the failure to perform is just as much a real damage as the destruction or appro-

[1] *Ibid.*, p. 40.

[2] *Civilrechtliche Erörterungen: I. Vorverhandlungen bei Verträgen,* Weimar, 1868.

[3] *Ibid.*, p. 20.

[4] *Der Vertrag*, Leipzig, 1876.

priation of another's property. There is no reason for any legal distinction between the cases.

The reason why the author of an express or tacit promise is considered bound to compensate the damage caused to the promisee by non-performance, is to be found in the universal principle, which is contained in our immediate jural consciousness, and which, requiring no proof, is to be regarded as an axiom: that whoever culpably causes damage to another is in duty bound to compensate such damage.[1]

In order to justify the decisions of the Roman jurists quoted by Savigny, he holds that these passages have been torn out of their proper context, and that we must read into them the necessity of knowledge of the mistake by the other party, although this knowledge may sometimes be dispensed with upon proof that the mistake was excusable.[2] His theory may be called the damage or failure of performance theory.

Another aspect of the objective theory is presented by Schall,[3] whose views may be called the positive law theory of the juristic act. "Neither the intention nor the will of the party, but, as the word *Rechtsgeschäft* would signify, the will of the law gives to an act the characteristic of a juristic act."[4] Once a declaration is made, the law will attach to it the proper legal consequences without reference to the will of the party.[5] Mistake (*unrichtige Vorstellung*) in Schall's opinion can have no effect. The party making a declaration through mistake must be held responsible for such declaration according to the content which the law reads into it, entirely independently of his real will.[6]

[1] *Ibid.*, pp. 288, 289.
[2] *Ibid.*, p. 115. [3] *Der Parteiwille im Rechtsgeschäft*, Stuttgart, 1877.
[4] *Ibid.*, p. 5. [5] *Ibid.*, p. 22. [6] *Ibid.*, pp. 41, 42.

A doctrine which accepts Savigny's position as fundamental, but proposes improvements in its theoretical statement, is that of Zitelmann.[1] It demands careful attention because of its logical analysis of the function of mistake.[2] Mistake is to Zitelmann simply a "*Moment*," possessing a positive and negative side. When the correct view of the situation ("*wahre Vorstellung*") is "*Thatbestandsmoment*," the function of mistake is always negative, *i. e.*, the "*irrige Vorstellung*," or mistake, will result in nullity. But when the "*irrige Vorstellung*" is "*Thatbestandsmoment*," the function of mistake is always positive, *i. e.*, it is only the "*irrige Vorstellung*" which produces any legal result. In the first class of cases, the law requires the existence of the "*wahre Vorstellung*," *i. e.*, a correct view, and since it is supplanted by the "*irrige Vorstellung*," *i. e.*, a mistaken view, the law decrees nullity. In the second class of cases, it is the "*irrige Vorstellung*," *i. e.*, the mistaken concept, which the law requires in order to produce legal consequences. The law does not require that the party shall make a mistake; it requires mistake only in the sense that mistake is in fact the foundation of ensuing rights and liabilities.[3]

Zitelmann has made a careful investigation of the psychological nature of mistake.[4] He concludes that mistake exists in but three forms, *viz.*, in consciousness, in intent, and in motive. In each of these forms mistake exercises, at least theoretically, its positive and negative functions.[5] Concretely, a mistake in consciousness is a mistake as to the *Thun*, or proper act. A mistake in intention is a mistake as to the *Folge*, or consequences of the *Thun*. A mis-

[1] *Irrthum und Rechtsgeschäft*, 1879. [2] *Cf.* especially pp. 6–8.
[3] *Ibid.*, pp. 343–354. [4] *Ibid.*, pp. 1–196. [5] *Ibid.*, pp. 346, 347.

take in motive explains itself.[1] While mistake has theoretically a positive and negative function in each of these forms, yet in reality it discharges a negative function in the first two forms only, *i. e.,* in the act and its consequences. In the third form, *i. e.,* in motive, mistake can really exercise only a positive function.[2] It thus appears that Zitelmann's positive and negative functions of mistake correspond exactly with Savigny's *echt* and *unecht* classes of mistake, save that Zitelmann would treat mistake *in substantia* as a mistake in motive. Zitelmann thus avoids the disadvantages of Savigny's terminology, and at the same time presents a logical basis for the fundamental distinction established by Savigny.[3]

Hesse, who originated the idea of a positive and negative function of mistake,[4] failed to work out the true distinction as formulated by Zitelmann. Hesse thinks that a mistake in motive may be a ground of nullity whenever the motive, according to the concept or nature of the juristic act, or according to its recognizable content, appears as a legal *Moment* of the act.[5] Hesse probably means by this that some mistakes in motive are to be considered as negative *Thatbestandsmomente.* In other words, a mistake in motive is a ground of nullity whenever such a mistake excludes the real will. This is apparently a contradiction. The condition is conceivable, but it would also seem extremely difficult of realization. Hesse's doctrine is otherwise the same as Zitelmann's. He was led to his conclusions because of his disagreement with the tenet of the

[1] *Ibid.*, p. 340. [2] *Ibid.*, p. 357.

[3] *Ibid.*, p. 350. *Cf.* an earlier exposition of the theory by Zitelmann, "Die juristische Willenserklarüng," in *Jahrbücher für Dogmatik*, xvi, pp. 357–436.

[4] "Eine Revision der Lehre von Irrthum" in *Jahrbücher für Dogmatik*, xv, pp. 62–135. [5] *Ibid.*, p. 78.

subjective theory, that mistake could not *per se* cause nullity, and that a mistake in motive is immaterial.[1]

Voigt[2] would classify mistake with reference to the expression of the will, the motive, the *causa*, and the determination or fixing of the will. The distinction between these categories is not made clear. He insists throughout that the extent of the mistake, the degree in which wills and declarations differ, is practically the decisive point.

Bekker[3] presents two leading thoughts. First, it is an indispensable prerequisite to the validity of a juristic act that its consequences be appreciated. He, therefore, separates mistakes which exclude a true will into two classes, *viz.*, mistake as to the act itself and mistake as to its consequences.[4] Second, since a declaration implies a corresponding will, the declaration which does not correspond to the will is abnormal.[5] Bekker's distinction between normal and abnormal declarations is not to be confused with Savigny's distinction between *echter* and *unechter Irrthum*. Bekker's abnormal class covers the whole field included by Savigny in both classes. Not all abnormal declarations, he says, are invalid in Roman law, but the Romans themselves formulated no general principle; "in single cases they adroitly determined the results of mistake so as to meet the needs of daily life."[6] Bekker's views have not been widely accepted.

[1] *Cf.* an earlier discussion by Hesse in *Archiv für civilistische Praxis*, liii, pp. 182 *et seq.*

[2] "Die Theorie von der juristischen Relevanz von *error* und *ignorantia*," in *Archiv für civil. Praxis*, liii, pp. 405–436; liv, pp. 23–80, 194–241.

[3] "Zur civilistischen Literatur," *Kritische Vierteljahrsschrift*, iii, pp. 187–202.

[4] *Ibid.*, iii, pp. 192–197.

[5] *Ibid.*, iii, p. 195. *Cf.* also *ibid.*, v, p. 396.

[6] *Ibid.*, iii, p. 201.

Hölder[1] regards Bekker's analysis of mistake, *viz.*, mistake as to the act itself and mistake as to its consequences, as meritorious, but he attempts to push the analysis further. In his view there are three important classes of cases. The declaration itself may so deviate from the will that there is really no act. The result in this case is, of course, nullity. Or, secondly, the declaration may have failed to convey to the person to whom it is addressed the real will of the declarant. In contracts, the result is nullity because of *dissensus*. Finally, the declaration may have been willed, but not its content. A mistake of this character does not make the act void, but it may enable the mistaken party to repudiate his declaration. In other words, a mistake as to content may make the act voidable.[2]

Dernburg does not accept, in their extreme forms, either the subjective or the objective theory, but suggests an intermediate ground.[3] As to gifts and testaments, he would enforce the will theory absolutely. In other cases he would make a concession, on account of the *Verkehrsinteresse* and also on the ground of negligence. He rather approves of Hartmann's position.[4] In place of the term "*unechter Irrthum*" he would substitute "*Geschäftsirrthum*," or mistake in the act, as more appropriate.

French writers and courts adhere to the subjective theory with certain modifications of an equitable nature to be noticed later.[5] It is clear that Hartmann is unjustified in attempting to found his argument upon French cases. Those quoted by him depend upon section 1321 of the

[1] "Die Lehre vom *error*," *Kritische Vierteljahrsschrift*, xiv, pp. 561–583.

[2] *Ibid.*, pp. 580, 581.

[3] *Pandekten*, i, p. 229.

[4] *Ibid.*, p. 227 n. 1.

[5] Pothier, *Oeuvres*, vol. xiv, pp. 597, 598. See also vol. i, pp. 92–94. Dalloz, *Jurisprudence Générale*, xxxiii, secs. 111–167, pp. 79–89.

French code, which provides that collateral writings (*contre-lettres*) shall affect the rights of the contracting parties only, and not those of third persons. Such collateral evidence would, for example, have no operation against an assignee or a *bona fide* purchaser for value. It is obvious that decisions rendered on such a ground do not substantiate Hartmann's position.

The subjective theory of contract and the operation of mistake under this theory have been sufficiently set forth above, in connection with the doctrine of Savigny. A passing notice is all that is needed as regards its modern supporters. Thus, Wendt approves of the subjective theory as such, but urges that " in matters of practical law it is frequently indispensable to discard the strict logical consequence and to recognize exceptions to the rule for the sake of justice." [1] Puchta accepts Savigny's theory in its entirety.[2] Vangerow supports the will theory, but interprets the phrase "*nulla errantis voluntas est*" in its literal sense, and thus applies it to the *unecht* class.[3] While he may attain, to a certain extent, the same results, yet his theory is illogical when brought into contact with the doctrine of *dolus*. Baron adds a fourth class of mistake, *i. e.*, as to the will of the other party.[4] This distinction, however, is superfluous, for such a mistake would regularly result in a *dissensus*. Böcking clearly stands for the will theory, although he does not appear to recognize the distinction between the *echt* and *unecht* classes.[5] Eck also supports the subjective theory, but would amplify Savigny's classification of essential mistakes by distinguishing between mistake as to the act itself and as to the results of the act.[6] This distinction has al-

[1] *Pandekten*, p. 114.
[2] *Pandekten*, i, pp. 100–104.
[3] *Pandekten*, i, pp. 118–120.
[4] *Pandekten*, p. 83.
[5] *Pandekten*, i, p. 297.
[6] "Irrthum im Civilrecht," in Holtzendorff's *Rechtslexikon*, pp. 399–402.

ready been noted above in connection with Hölder's views. Goldschmidt would protect equities which the prevailing doctrine fails to reach.[1] Brinz differs from Savigny mainly in admitting an absolute nullity only when the declaration itself is not willed.[2] Thibaut would refuse to recognize nullity when the mistake is due to gross negligence.[3] Unger follows Savigny, criticizing the Austrian code, which excludes consideration of mistake unless it was known to the other party.[4] Arndt also supports the subjective theory, although he disapproves of Savigny's terminology.[5] Wächter follows Savigny closely.[6] Windscheid, as we have seen, approves Savigny's fundamental distinction, although he rejects Savigny's nomenclature.[7]

The majority of the criticisms noted in this chapter are based on Savigny's failure to recognize the equities of the innocent party who takes a declaration at its face value. The efforts of jurists, courts and legislators to satisfy these equities will be noticed in the following chapters; and it will be shown that such efforts do not require the abandonment of Savigny's theory. That theory must be accepted as fundamental. It may be modified or improved, but it cannot be rejected or supplanted by any of the foregoing theories of mistake. The comparison almost speaks for itself. As regards the Roman law, at least, Windscheid is right in saying: "The grounds which have been presented in favor of these new principles are not tenable, and they are contradicted by the passages in the Digest which bear upon the subject of mistake." [8]

[1] Goldschmidt, *Handelsrecht*, pp. 547, 548.

[2] *Cf.* Mandry's review of Brinz's *Pandekten* in *Kritische Vierteljahrsschrift*, xiv, p. 378.

[3] *Pandekten*, ii, p. 7, sec. 448.

[4] *System des österreichischen allgemeinen Privatrechts*, ii, p. 125.

[5] *Pandekten*, i, p. 75.

[6] *Würtemburgisches Privatrecht*, ii, p. 743.

[7] *Pandekten*, i, sec. 76 *et seq.*

[8] *Ibid.*, (5th ed.), i, sec. 75, n. 1a. *Cf.* Wendt, *Pandekten*, p. 113.

CHAPTER III

Negligence and Excusability

Probably no better illustration could be given of a complete change in ideas than the treatment of the subjects of negligence and excusability in the German draft and final codes. According to Savigny, nullity results from the absence of an intention corresponding to the declaration independently of the question of negligence or excusability. The draft code drew a distinction between ordinary and gross negligence.[1] It imposed nullity, in section 98, whenever the will and expression disagreed, but in section 99 it excluded this result when the mistaken party was guilty of gross negligence. In the case of ordinary negligence, nullity was to follow, but compensation was to be awarded to the party who had suffered damage by reason of his reliance on the declaration ("negative damages"). The corresponding section of the code as adopted allows acts to be set aside because of mistake, without regard to negligence, whether gross or ordinary, but awards compensation ("negative damages") to the party who is entitled to rely on the declaration.[2] The discussion of the draft code brought out many valuable contributions to the theory of mistake, and the reasons advanced for and against the consideration of negligence and excusability are very instructive.

The motives accompanying the draft code explain why the commission departed from the usual rule and enforced

[1] *Entwurf eines bürgerlichen Gesetzbuchs*, secs. 98, 99.

[2] *Bürgerliches Gesetzbuch*, secs. 119, 122.

the contract in the case of gross negligence.[1] The reason assigned was that if one lays aside all customary care and makes a declaration which does not correspond with his real will, he ought not to complain when such declaration is treated as the expression of his actual will. This argument was overruled in many of the opinions elicited by the draft code, on the ground that both the nullity of the contract and the duty to compensate the other party arise independently of all negligence. In the final revision of the code this criticism was recognized as valid, and negligence disappeared as an element in the production of the juristic act or contract. The result is a singular vindication of the views of Savigny upon this point. The new element, both in the draft code and in the code as adopted, is the recognition of the equities of the other party according to the theory of "negative interest," which will be described later.

Among the opinions (*Gutachten*) submitted while the draft code was under consideration, and subsequently digested by the imperial department of justice, the following relate to the question of negligence and excusability.

Hachenburg, who insisted that the will was always present, though defective, even in the *unecht* class of mistake, and that the act was merely voidable (*anfechtbar*), was unwilling to draw any distinction between ordinary and gross negligence.[2] Such a distinction, he argued, is impracticable, as well as incorrect in principle. If the result is to depend on whether the mistaken party was at fault or not, there would be numerous cases in which it would be necessary to assume the existence of such fault or negligence when in fact there is none. The rule proposed by Hachenburg is that an act is voidable provided it has been induced

[1] *Motive zu dem Entwurf eines bürgerl. Gesetzbuchs*, i, p. 200.

[2] *Gutachtliche Aeusserungen zu dem Entwurf, etc.*, i, p. 169.

by an essential mistake, and provided further that the other party could have noticed the mistake under the peculiar circumstances of the particular case.

Heinsheimer approved of the distinction between gross and ordinary negligence, because thereby the demands of commercial intercourse and the requirements of daily life are best satisfied.[1]

Unger disapproved very strongly of the delict or tort standpoint of the draft code.[2] While adhering to the subjective theory, he would always protect the equities ("negative interest") of the other party. This negative interest must always exist without reference to the question whether the mistaken party is or is not guilty of negligence. To say that an act shall depend for its validity upon the question whether or not the mistaken party was guilty of negligence is unfair, because it tends to put the damage upon the other party, who may be absolutely innocent. Every one must act on his own responsibility. It is unworthy of an upright man to put the disadvantage arising from his act upon the other party. Unger, therefore, declared that the particular provision in the draft code was mere pedantry, unsuited to actual requirements, and that such a provision must lead to great uncertainty in practice, because of the difficulty of determining what is gross as distinguished from ordinary negligence. He admitted that the subjective theory protects the mistaken party at the expense of the other. But the objective theory goes to the other extreme by enforcing the contract against the mistaken party. Such absolute liability overreaches the mark. It is sufficient that the deceived party be kept free from damage. The act must be treated as null for essential mistake, and the other party must be protected by a claim for negative damages.

[1] *Gutachten*, i, p. 166. [2] *Ibid.*, i, p. 166.

For these reasons Unger disapproved of the recognition, in the draft code, of the element of negligence in the matter of mistake.

Gierke agreed largely with Unger.[1] In answering the question how far one party is to be protected against the mistake of the other, it is immaterial, he argued, whether and in what degree the mistaken party was negligent. The mistaken party is not to be punished according to the degree of his negligence. All that the other party can require is that the mistaken party shall bear the consequent damage arising through the nullity of the contract. The right to compensation arises not out of the validity of the declaration, nor out of the negligence of the mistaken party, but only out of the duty of such mistaken party to make good the damage ensuing from his mistake. Hence, there is no reason for insisting upon a distinction between gross and ordinary negligence, nor for considering negligence as an element at all.

Planck was inclined to think that consideration ought to be given to the question of negligence in determining the extent of the duty to pay negative damages.[2] The usual question in cases of mistake is: Which of the two parties shall bear the loss? This question, Planck urged, should be stated differently, as follows: Does a sufficient ground exist to justify the other party in putting the damage on the mistaken party? He argued that while negligence may have degrees, the lack of it, or innocence, cannot. He, therefore, regarded negligence as a necessary element in determining the duty to pay negative damages.

Bähr, representing the objective theory, insisted upon the absolute protection of commercial interests (*Verkehrsinteressen*).[3] He was unwilling to lay any weight upon the sub-

[1] *Gutachten*, i, p. 167. [2] *Ibid.*, i, p. 167. [3] *Ibid.*, i, pp. 166, 167.

jective negligence of the mistaken party. It does not matter whether such party is negligent or not when the object is the protection of *bona fide* transactions. The distinction between ordinary and gross negligence is of doubtful expediency, because of the difficulty in differentiating the degrees, and unjust, because the other party cannot know all the circumstances under which the declaration is given, and therefore cannot make the necessary distinction in his own behalf. Bähr was inclined to think that the enforcement of the contract really amounts to nothing more than the protection of the other party from positive harm. If this were not the fact, he would favor a return to the subjective theory as defended by his opponents.

Independently of the discussion of the draft code, the question of excusability of mistake had received due attention in the juristic literature.

Dernburg takes issue with Savigny on this point. He interprets the Roman law as holding that nullity cannot follow when the mistake is inexcusable. His reason for requiring a consideration of negligence is that otherwise a premium would be put upon it. He, however, admits that in the Prussian law, except in the case of *error in substantia*, an inexcusable mistake does not stand in the way of nullity.[1]

Hesse, on the contrary, is of the opinion that the question of negligence is absolutely immaterial. It can make no difference whether the mistake is inexcusable or not. Even when it is inexcusable and easy to avoid, there is still wanting the vital element of will.[2] Sohm, who treats *error in substantia* as mistake in motive, would relieve against it only when it is excusable.[3] Zitelmann admits that his

[1] Dernburg, *Pandekten*, i, p. 233; *Preussisches Privatrecht*, i, p. 231.

[2] Hesse, "Eine Revision der Lehre vom Irrthum," in *Jahrbücher für Dogmatik*, xv, pp. 62–135.

[3] Sohm, *Institutes*, translated by Ledlie, sec. 42, pp 221 *et seq.*

theory of a negative function of mistake, if carried out to its ultimate results, would, like Savigny's theory, ignore the element of excusability. Nullity would, therefore, follow even though the mistake was inexcusable. But Zitelmann is unwilling to admit such a consequence when the mistake is inexcusable. He proposes, accordingly, to treat inexcusable mistake not as an *irrige Vorstellung*, but as an alternative *Thatbestandsmoment*, producing validity equally with the *wahre Vorstellung*.[1] This construction is, of course, inconsistent with his theory of the negative function of mistake. It constitutes an exception to his general rule.

In the earlier editions of his *Pandects*, Windscheid followed Savigny in this matter. " Mistake," he wrote, " is merely the reason why that which is not really willed is declared as willed. From this follows the important rule that the nullity of the declaration is not excluded because the mistake is inexcusable." [2] In later editions, however, he recognized that the prevailing theory was to the contrary; and in the last edition, published while the debates on the draft code were in progress, he declared that a mistake due to gross negligence could not be considered in any case, and that in the field of contracts a mistake could not operate to invalidate the transaction unless it were excusable. Both of these rules, however, he regarded as exceptions to the general principle.[3]

Goldschmidt would seem to regard excusability as a necessary element.[4] Wächter states that when the conditions of validity of the juristic act are absent, the subjects of negligence and excusability are not involved.[5] Vangerow holds

[1] Zitelmann, *Irrthum und Rechtsgeschäft*, p. 348.

[2] Windscheid, *Pandekten* (4th ed., 1875), i, pp. 199, 200.

[3] *Ibid.*, (7th ed., 1891), i, p. 197, n. 1d; p. 201.

[4] Goldschmidt, *Handelsrecht*, ii, p. 34.

[5] Wächter, *Württembürgisches Privatrecht*, ii, p. 743.

the same views.[1] Wendt thinks that justice requires some consideration of negligence and excusability, although nullity is the logical consequence of essential mistake.[2]

The position taken on this question by earlier codes is as follows.

The Prussian *Landrecht* provides that nullity shall follow, although the mistake was inexcusable. Compensation must be made to an innocent party who suffers by the mistake; but if both parties are guilty of an inexcusable mistake, neither can have compensation.[3] The French civil code makes no allusion to the question of negligence in the matter of mistake.[4] The civil code of Saxony excludes all consideration of negligence.[5]

To the writer it seems that the doctrine of Savigny is the correct one as regards the matter of negligence and excusability. These are properly immaterial elements. Any injustice which results from this construction is eliminated by the doctrine of negative interest, to be noticed later.

[1] Vangerow, *Pandekten*, i, p. 120.

[2] Wendt, *Pandekten*, p. 114.

[3] *Allgemeines Landrecht* (ed. Koch), i, secs. 78–80.

[4] *Code Civil*, secs. 1108–1110.

[5] *Sächsisches Gesetzbuch*, sec. 843.

CHAPTER IV

Essentiality of Mistake

Savigny adopted no single general principle of essentiality, but concluded, from an examination of the Roman law, that the cases could be classified as mistakes with respect to the nature of the legal relationship, the identity of the person or thing, and the quality of the thing. In all these instances there is an objective standard. The authors of the German draft code sought to improve upon this, and adopted the so-called subjective standard. The draft code provided that whenever the lack of agreement between the real will and the declared will is due to a mistake, "the declaration is void, if it is to be assumed that the declarant, had he been aware of the actual situation, would not have made the declaration." Mistakes regarding the nature of the transaction, the object of the transaction and the persons affected were then mentioned as special cases, in which it was to be presumed that the declaration would not have been made but for the mistake.[1]

This provision elicited varying opinions. Hölder argued that concessions ought not to be made to the individual situation and views of the declarant, except in so far as they can be known to the other party.[2] Jacoby disapproved of the provision for the same reason.[3] Schilling pronounced

[1] *Entwurf*, sec. 98. *Cf. Motive*, i, p. 198. It should be noted that this section, with its subjective standard, applied only to mistakes which exclude a corresponding will, and not to mistakes in motive. Section 102 laid down the general rule that mistakes in motives are immaterial.

[2] *Gutachten*, i, p. 170. [3] *Ibid.*, i, p. 170.

the subjective standard uncertain and indefinite. Advocating the rule that persons competent to act should be held to their declarations, unless their mistakes are capable of being known to the other party, he believed that exceptions to this rule should be limited rather than extended; but the effect of the provision in the draft code would be to extend them.[1] Leonhard repudiated the subjective standard, partly because, if it were rigidly enforced, almost any declaration could be held void, and partly because the court would be required to act upon a very indefinite subject-matter. The standard of essentiality can only be fixed by the experience of honest men through commercial customs. When such a standard has been established, a party knows exactly what he has to expect when an offer is made: he knows what kind of mistake may invalidate the contract.[2]

On the other hand, Heinsheimer supported the subjective standard.[3] Hachenburg thought that the question of essentiality should be determined according to the peculiar circumstances of each case. Due consideration should be given to the standpoint of the declarant, but the question should be left almost entirely to the discretion of the court. This would remove the necessity of a statutory definition of essentiality. Hachenburg, however, would insist in every case that the mistake be capable of being detected by the other party.[4] Hellmann admitted that the rule proposed in the draft code was apparently simple, but thought that upon closer approach all the old disputes would be raised anew in its interpretation.[5]

In the final revision of the code the subjective standard of essentiality was retained, except as regards mistake *in substantia*. The provision of the code as adopted upon this point is as follows:

[1] *Gutachten*, i, p. 170.
[2] *Ibid.*, p. 170.
[3] *Ibid.*, pp. 170, 171.
[4] *Ibid.*, p. 170.
[5] *Ibid.*, p. 171.

Whoever, in making a declaration of will, was in error as to its content, or did not at all intend to make a declaration of such content, can attack the declaration if it is to be assumed that with knowledge of the situation and with an intelligent consideration of the case he would not have made the declaration.

Equivalent to mistake as to the content of the declaration is the mistake concerning such properties of the person or thing as in ordinary dealings are regarded as essential.[1]

The difficulty in detecting essential mistake, and especially in differentiating it from mistake in motive, may be illustrated by the following case. The plaintiff in Hamburg insured a cotton factory in Japan, and then reinsured the whole amount, placing two-fifths with the defendant in Aix. After loss by fire, and upon consequent suit, the defendant alleged essential mistake as a defense, in that he had supposed the reinsurance to be only partial. The plaintiff won his case in first instance, was defeated upon appeal, and upon further appeal secured again a decision in his favor. The case was governed by French law. The court of second instance held that the mistake came within the provisions of article 1110 of the French civil code, inasmuch as it related to the nature of the object of the contract. The court of final resort reversed this decision, holding that the mistake was purely in motive.[2]

Another case which illustrates the same point, and also the relation between mistake in motive and fraud, arose in Offenburg. The plaintiff, who was in a manufacturing business with his son-in-law, sold out his interest to the latter and the defendant jointly, and then brought suit for the purchase price. The property was in fact so encum-

[1] *Bürgerliches Gesetzbuch*, sec. 119. The provision of the draft code as to mistake in motive has disappeared.

[2] *Entscheidungen des Reichsgerichts in Civilsachen*, liii, p. 138 (1902).

bered as to be worthless. The defense pleaded was essential mistake, and judgment was given accordingly. Upon appeal, the court expressly overruled this defense, but affirmed the decision on the ground of fraud.[1]

In another case the plaintiff sought a divorce from his wife, who at the time of marriage was already pregnant by another man. The basis of the application was essential mistake. The court refused relief because the mistake was not as to the person, but only as to a characteristic.[2] There was, however, a divergence of views upon this question.

Another case of very recent date was based on the purchase by the plaintiff of a license to manufacture from March 27, 1900, up to December 31, 1904. As a fact, the government patent had expired on February 18, 1904, and the plaintiff sought to set the contract aside for essential mistake upon this point, under section 119 of the German imperial code. The court held that the ground of relief must be, not that of mistake, but that of impossibility of performance, under section 307.[3]

In another case, the plaintiff had contracted to deliver 500 pieces of cloth to a certain firm, and had delivered 404 pieces when the firm became bankrupt. Under section 17 of the bankruptcy law, the administrator had the option of closing the transaction or of demanding full performance; but in the latter case the plaintiff would be entitled to full payment. The defendant, appointed as administrator, called for delivery of the cloth due under the contract without knowledge of the fact that the cloth for which he was calling was part of a large amount, the bulk of which had been delivered, or of the fact that no payment had yet

[1] *Entscheidungen des Reichsoberhandelsgerichts*, v, p. 70 (1872).

[2] *Entscheidungen des Reichsgerichts in Civilsachen*, xxiii, p. 332 (1889).

[3] *Ibid.*, li, p. 92 (1902).

been made by the bankrupt firm for the goods previously delivered. On receipt of defendant's demand for the balance of the cloth due, the plaintiff demanded payment. The defendant immediately replied that he had acted under a mistake, and withdrew his demand for the balance of the cloth. The plaintiff then sued for payment, and in the original and appellate instances the decision was in favor of the defendant. The appellate court based its decision on section 119 of the imperial civil code, declaring that the defendant acted under an essential mistake as to the object of his declaration. He intended only to secure 96 pieces of cloth, not to make the bankrupt estate liable for full payment for 500 pieces. The supreme court of the empire held that this reasoning was erroneous. There was no mistake as to the object of the declaration, but only as to the legal consequences of the declaration. The supreme court, however, suggested that a demand for the performance of a contract supposed to be entire was a different thing from a demand for the completion of the performance of a more extensive contract. If mistake were proven on this point, it could be regarded as a mistake in respect to the content of the declaration. Accordingly the case was sent back for re-examination of the evidence, in order to ascertain whether such a mistake in respect to the content of the declaration could be regarded as established.[1]

Before the first draft of the German civil code was published, and independently of the opinions elicited by its provisions, the standard of essentiality of mistake was the subject of no little discussion.

Zitelmann objects to Savigny's treatment of essential mistake, because it is based on no single principle. Savigny's classes have presented themselves in the light of experience

[1] *Ibid.*, li, p. 281 (1902).

as the most frequently occurring cases. The classification is, therefore, neither exhaustive nor correct. The correct principle, Zitelmann thinks, consists in the individualization of the intention with respect to any given point. If this condition is present, the mistake is essential, otherwise not. He urges that every possible basis of a juristic act, so far as mistake is concerned, is of the same legal importance. He would always ask whether the intention was directed toward the particular point. If so, a mistake as to such point is essential, otherwise not. Under such a rule, mistakes as to time, place, circumstance, and many other points commonly regarded as unessential, may be treated as essential.[1]

Dernburg, in his presentation of modern Roman law, holds that a mistake is essential when, according to common experience, it can be seen that the mistaken party would not have made the contract had he possessed a clear conception of the facts.[2] Wendt criticizes the rule laid down by Dernburg, on the ground that it tends to include mistake in motive.[3]

Leonhard, as previously noted, holds that a mistake is essential whenever it relates to circumstances of which the existence was discernibly an implied condition precedent. If the particular point concerning which there is a mistake is not important, *i. e.*, if it is not apparent or deducible from the declarations of the parties that a correct conception was requisite touching the particular point or circumstance in regard to which a mistake exists, then the mistake is not essential, or rather it is to be treated as not existing, so far as the validity of the contract is concerned.[4]

[1] Zitelmann, *Irrthum und Rechtsgeschäft*, pp. 491–496.

[2] Dernburg, *Pandekten*, i, p. 234. [3] Wendt, *Pandekten*, p. 115.

[4] Leonhard, *Der Irrthum*, p. 570.

Eck thinks that the cases of essential mistake are manifold. The main or most important cases are those indicated by Savigny, but he would add mistake as to the content of the act, and as to time and place of performance.[1] Wächter and Windscheid adhere to Savigny's classification.[2]

The attitude of the earlier codes on this question is as follows: The Prussian *Landrecht* treats as essential such mistakes as relate to the character of the act or its chief object, the identity of the person when a particular person is intended, and characteristics of the thing or person when these are expressly indicated or impliedly presupposed according to the general usages of trade and intercourse.[3] The Austrian [4] and Saxon [5] codes designate practically the same classes, although, as already noted, the Austrian code permits mistake to be pleaded only when it was known to the other party.[6] The French code provides that a mistake is not a ground of nullity, unless it relates to the very substance of the thing which is the object of the contract. It is not a cause of nullity when it concerns the person with whom one intends to contract, unless the consideration of such person constitutes the principal ground for making the contract.[7] The provisions of the Italian code are substantially identical with those of the French code.[8]

It will be seen that the new German code stands alone in making the standard of essentiality subjective.

[1] "Irrthum im Civilrecht," Holtzendorff, *Rechtslexikon*, p. 400.

[2] Windscheid, *Pandekten*, i, sec. 76. Wächter, *Würtemburgisches Privatrecht*, ii, pp. 743–749.

[3] *Allgemeines Landrecht*, i, 4, secs. 75–77. *Cf.* Dernburg, *Preussisches Privatrecht*, i, p. 229.

[4] *Oesterreichisches Gesetzbuch*, secs. 871 *et seq.* *Cf.* Unger, *Oesterreichisches Privatrecht*, ii, p. 125.

Sächsisches Gesetzbuch, secs. 95 *et seq.*, 838 *et seq.*

[6] Except as regards marriage; see *Oesterreichisches Gesetzbuch*, sec. 57.

[7] *Code Civil*, secs. 1110, 2053, 180. [8] *Codice Civile*, sec. 1110.

CHAPTER V

Error in Substantia

In the motives to the German draft code it was suggested that mistake *in substantia* might advantageously be treated as mistake in motive.[1] Objection was made to the principle laid down by Savigny upon this point—that mistake *in substantia* was to be regarded as an essential variation between declaration and intention—on account of the difficulty of fixing definite rules of practice. If mistake *in substantia* were treated as mistake in motive, the mistaken party could obtain relief without treating the act as void. Reference was made in particular to guarantees against defects in a thing, according to the provisions of section 381 *et seq.* of the draft code; to the remedies in case of fraud or other wilful wrong, according to the provisions of sections 103, 704 and 705; and to the effect given to tacit conditions in section 137. The chief section concerning mistake, however, as Meischeider [2] pointed out, was not framed in accordance with this recommendation. The adoption of the subjective standard of essentiality (in section 98) admitted mistake regarding essential characteristics. Leonhard [3] approved of this result, because such a mistake, in his opinion, is very essential and cannot be treated as a mere matter of motive. In its final revision, the German civil code follows Savigny's rule. Mistake regarding such properties of the person or thing as in ordinary dealings are regarded as

[1] *Motive zu dem Entwurf*, i, p. 199. [2] *Gutachten*, i, p. 171.

[3] *Ibid.*, i, p. 171.

essential is made equivalent to mistake as to the content of the declaration.[1]

Savigny's rule regarding mistake *in substantia* is adopted and interpreted in the following decisions:

The plaintiff bought shares in a stock company which, according to the terms of a prospectus, was to be formed for the purpose of purchasing a manufactory for 1,200,000 thalers. It afterwards appeared that the promoter kept for himself, as compensation for his efforts in bringing about the organization, the sum of 100,000 thalers. The plaintiff insisted that he was ignorant of this latter fact, and sought to escape from his contract on the ground that a mistake as to real value was the same as a mistake *in substantia.* The court, however, held that the intention to buy the particular shares was unquestionable, and that a mistake as to value was merely a mistake in motive.[2]

In another case, the plaintiff bought a piece of land for building purposes in the city of Bockenheim for 600 marks, believing that the street assessments which he assumed were only 530 marks. In fact, these assessments amounted to 3,680 marks, and permission to build was denied by the authorities until this latter amount was paid. The *Landgericht* of Frankfort held that the plaintiff could not escape from his contract because, as it appeared, he had accepted conveyance with previous knowledge that there were assessments. The *Oberlandesgericht* reversed this judgment, holding that the mistake was an essential one *in substantia,* because it affected the availability of the land for building purposes (*Bauqualität*). The *Reichsgericht* reversed the judgment of the intermediate instance and followed Savigny's doctrine, citing his exact words. Such a mistake

[1] *Bürgerliches Gesetzbuch*, sec. 119.

[2] *Entscheidungen des Reichsoberhandelsgerichts*, xxii, p. 388 (1877).

as this, it declared, was a clear mistake in motive. There was no mistake whatever *in substantia*, since the object was what it was supposed to be. Nullity of the contract, therefore, could not follow.[1]

In another case the defendant sold some cotton at Amsterdam, which turned out to be of a grade inferior to that which the plaintiffs expected. They thereupon sought to repudiate the purchase. The court said that this was not a mistake *in substantia* within the rule as laid down by Savigny. A mistake in quality as such is really a mistake in motive and will not entail nullity. The article must be something essentially different from what it was mistakenly supposed to be. A mere difference in grade or degree will not satisfy the requirements of the rule, and in the absence of a warranty the plaintiffs were not entitled to relief.[2]

There has been no little discussion of this topic in the German legal literature. Hesse disagrees with Savigny.

> Mistake in the quality of an object, even though essential, cannot lead to nullity of the declaration, because when one has willed the object his declaration corresponds with his will. One does not usually intend the quality, but a definite thing or class of things to which he attributes certain qualities, and which he may intend because he attributes to it such qualities.[3]

Nullity must follow when the will is directed to a certain thing, or to a certain species or kind of thing, and when this will is not truly expressed by the declaration. But nullity cannot follow when the mistake concerns the mere qualities of the thing. Such a mistake, to use Savigny's terminology, is an *echter Irrthum*.[4]

[1] *Entscheidungen des Reichsgerichts in Civilsachen*, xix, p. 260 (1888).

[2] *Entscheidungen des Reichsoberhandelsgerichts*, vii, p. 1.

[3] Hesse, "Eine Revision der Lehre vom Irrthum," *Jahrbücher für Dogmatik*, xv, p. 101.

[4] *Ibid.*, p. 105.

Zitelmann, in his own peculiar terminology, says the same thing. Mistake *in substantia* belongs to the class of mistakes which exercise, not a negative, but a positive function. The juristic act must be considered as actually produced, and the mistake operates positively as a ground of relief. His reason for this proposition is that individualization has already taken place with regard to a person or thing, when such person or thing is the object of the will. The attributes of such a person or thing do not constitute the object.[1] Wendt maintains that mistake *in substantia* is purely a mistake in motive, and is to be dealt with as such. The act, therefore, is merely voidable. He strongly disapproves of Savigny's view, and as strongly approves of Zitelmann's treatment of the subject.[2] Röver also regards a mistake *in substantia* as a mistake in motive.[3] Sohm treats mistake *in substantia* as mistake in motive, but would give relief against it, provided the mistake was excusable. This, in his opinion, is the doctrine of the Roman law, but he admits that the prevalent interpretation is to the contrary.[4] Pfersche would interpret Savigny as recognizing the proposition that a mistake *in substantia* is really a mistake in motive, although he treats it like mistake *in corpore*. A juristic act, Pfersche thinks, cannot be rendered null because of a mistake by the declarant regarding the quality or nature of the object of such act. Such a mistake is purely in motive.[5] He would lay down the following rule of practice: when the purchaser has made a mistake as to the properties or char-

[1] Zitelmann, *Irrthum und Rechtsgeschäft*, pp. 442–444, 490, 549.

[2] Wendt, *Pandekten*, pp. 102, 103.

[3] Röver, *Bedeutung des Willens*, p. 7.

[4] Sohm, *Institutes*, Ledlie's trans., pp. 220-222.

[5] Pfersche, *Zur Lehre vom sogenannten error in substantia* (Graz, 1880), pp. 5, 84, 99.

acter of the object, he can obtain relief by the *actio empti,* or action on the purchase, within definite limits, provided that the law does not directly decree that the act or contract in question shall be absolutely void.[1] Eck states that there is much dispute as to whether a mistake as to quality or character of person or thing is a sufficient ground of nullity, but he inclines toward Savigny's doctrine.[2] Dernburg favors the treatment adopted by Savigny as to mistake *in substantia,* but urges that in case of a pledge or pawn a mistake *in substantia* should not afford grounds of nullity, because it is better to get something than nothing.[3]

The provisions of some of the earlier codes upon this question are as follows. The Prussian *Landrecht* provides that mistake as to the characteristics commonly presupposed in a person or thing is a ground of nullity, except when the mistaken party was guilty of negligence.[4] The Saxon code accepts Savigny's rules.[5] The French code declares that mistake is a ground of nullity when it relates to "*la substance même de la chose.*[6] Pothier quotes a case of the purchase of a farm in a foreign country, when, just the day before the purchase, a hurricane had destroyed the buildings and trees upon it. The quality was, therefore, so far altered that the mistake could rightly be said to be as to the thing itself. But such a mistake could not be pleaded as to matters peculiarly within one's own knowledge nor when one might have easily learned the facts.[7]

[1] Pfersche, *Error in Substantia,* p. 48.

[2] "Irrthum in Civilrecht," in Holtzendorff, *Rechtslexikon,* p. 401.

[3] Dernburg, *Pandekten,* i, p. 237, and n. 13.

[4] *Allgemeines Landrecht,* secs. 77, 81, 82.

[5] *Sächsisches Gesetzbuch,* sec. 842.

[6] *Code Civil,* sec. 1110.

[7] Pothier, *Oeuvres,* i, pp. 92–94.

CHAPTER VI

Nullity or Voidability

The German draft code employed the words "null" and "nullity" (*nichtig* and *Nichtigkeit*) when dealing with acts which were declared to be invalid for essential mistake.[1] This was in accordance with the dominant theory, but the provision gave rise to some discussion. Hölder doubted whether absolute nullity of the juristic act on account of essential mistake was the best rule. It was more fitting, he thought, that the mistake of one party should afford no ground to the other for insisting upon nullity.[2] Unger favored "relative nullity" (*relative Nichtigkeit*). By this he meant a nullity which only the mistaken party could plead. The draft code, in section 110, permitted the author of a void act to confirm it, but treated such confirmation as a repetition of the act. Unger was unable to see why the mistaken party, who alone should be protected, should be prevented from letting the contract stand, in case this should be to his interest. No injustice could thereby befall the other party, since he had no reason to suppose that the contract was invalid. The other party may justly demand that he be protected against damage resulting from the mistake, but he cannot justly demand that he should draw advantage from it.[3] Heinsheimer thought that the question was a minor one, but favored the principle of a merely relative nullity.[4] Schilling called attention to the treatment of the cases of fraud and duress, in which, accord-

[1] *Entwurf*, sec. 98.

[2] *Gutachten*, i, p. 171. [3] *Ibid.* [4] *Ibid.*

ing to section 103 of the draft code, the act was not void, but merely "assailable" (*anfechtbar*). He argued that nullity in favor of the injured party would be much more justifiable in these cases than in the case of mistake which the other party was not to blame for and did not know.[1] Hachenburg, in accordance with his position that the will is not absent in the case of essential mistake but is merely defective, favored the term *Anfechtbarkeit*. Leonhard was disposed to avoid the term *Anfechtbarkeit*, because, although it settles nothing in regard to the cases of contract which are void *ab initio* for essential mistake, it attributes to the declaration a provisional validity.[2]

The jurists who asked for the recognition of a relative nullity in the case of essential mistake were not guilty of a confusion between void and voidable acts. When we use these terms we have two criteria of distinction. We say that an act is voidable when it can be attacked and invalidated by a certain person or certain persons only. We say, also, that an act is voidable when the attack upon the act and its recognition as invalid do not operate retroactively, so as to impair rights acquired in good faith by third persons. These criteria are usually combined. They may, however, be separated. The law may say that a certain person only can impugn the validity of an act, but that, when successfully impugned, the act shall be regarded as having been invalid *ab initio*. This is what the jurists above cited mean by "relative" nullity.

The code as adopted declares that acts done without serious intent, with a conscious variation between will and declaration, are in principle void (*nichtig*).[3] The only exception is that of the mental reservation.[4] Acts done under

[1] *Gutachten*, i, p. 171.

[2] *Ibid.*, i, p. 172.

[3] *Bürgerliches Gesetzbuch*, secs. 116–118.

[4] *Ibid.*, sec. 118.

essential mistake are declared to be "assailable" (*anfechtbar*).[1] The same is the case with acts induced by duress or fraud.[2] But the code further declares that if an assailable act is successfully assailed, it is to be regarded as void from the beginning.[3] This is, of course, relative nullity. The equities of third persons who were unaware of the mistake or duress or fraud, and who have suffered loss by the retroactive effect attributed to the declaration of nullity, are safeguarded by the rules regarding negative interest. Their equities rest, in all cases, on further contracts; and when these further contracts fail by reason of the annulment of the assailable contract on which they are founded, or by a resultant impossibility of performance, such third parties, if they were unaware of the mistake or fraud or duress, have a claim for negative damages against the parties with whom they contracted and on the validity of whose declarations they relied.

Superficially considered, section 119 appears to be a complete abandonment of Savigny's theory of the nature and effects of the *unechter Irrthum*, and also a partial abandonment of the subjective or will theory of the jural act. But when section 119 is taken in connection with section 142, it is clear that *Anfechtbarkeit* is something more than voidability, as we commonly use the word. The act behind which there is no corresponding will exists only as long as the mistaken party chooses to leave it unassailed, and when he assails it, it is as if it had never been at all. Fundamentally, Savigny's view has prevailed in this instance also; although, in this instance again, its failure to do justice to the equities of others has been corrected by the acceptance of Jhering's theory of negative interest.[4]

[1] *Bürgerliches Gesetzbuch*, sec. 119. [2] *Ibid.*, sec. 123. [3] *Ibid.*, sec. 142.

[4] *Cf.* Windscheid, *Pandekten* (8th ed.), i, p. 369, n. 2 (by Kipp), and p. 340, n. 4.

CHAPTER VII

JHERING'S NEGATIVE INTEREST IN CONTRACTS

IF the doctrine of Savigny be accepted, that nullity of the juristic act or contract must follow whenever an essential variation between the will and its expression can be shown, and if this is true independently of the question of negligence or excusability, as is undoubtedly the rule in the new German civil code as well as elsewhere, the hardship falling upon the other party, who very likely knew nothing and could be expected to know nothing of the mistake, is very great, and the injustice done him is very evident. The German law gave no relief in this respect until comparatively recent times. This very fact is cogent evidence of the absolute acceptance of the doctrine of Savigny in detail. The injustice of the situation, however, was recognized by Jhering, and to him the new civil code is indebted for appropriate provisions looking toward the recognition and protection of the clear equities of such innocent parties.[1]

Jhering's theory was not confined to cases where contracts were void because of essential variation between the will and the declaration of one of the parties; it included other cases. His chief contention was that every one was

[1] Jhering's theory was first stated in an article entitled "Culpa in contrahendo, oder Schadensersatz bei nichtigen oder nicht zur Perfektion gelangten Verträgen," in his *Jahrbücher*, iv, pp. 1–112. For a statement in English of Jhering's theory, see Munroe Smith, "Four German Jurists," *Political Science Quarterly*, xii, pp. 43–48.

under a duty in entering into a contract to assure himself that he was in a position to contract, as well as to take care that the contract was a valid one, so far as was within his power. In case of mistake, it is obviously the party making the mistake who has failed to discharge this duty.

The next question related to the measure of damages, in case they were allowed. Jhering was very particular in insisting that the damages should be measured, not by the interest which the other party might have in securing the performance of the contract, but only by the interest which he might possibly have in the validity of the contract as such. The party in question, he said, should have no claim either for the performance of the contract, or for damages for non-performance; for to allow either claim would be to recognize the invalid contract as valid. What should be accorded him is a claim to be put in as good a position as if he had never been led to suppose that he had a contract. This, as contrasted with the "positive interest" in performance, Jhering termed "negative interest." [1]

Savigny not only ignored the equities of the contracting party who had made no mistake and who could not but rely on the declaration of the other party, but he overlooked one class of cases in the Roman law, in which such a negative interest was recognized.[2] The discovery that there were such cases was made by Jhering, who produced them in support of his theory. He showed that such an interest was recognized in the case of the sale of an object which

[1] Munroe Smith, *loc. cit.*, p. 45.

[2] Windscheid, *Pandekten* (7th ed.), ii, sec. 307, n. 5, makes the assertion that Savigny recognized the doctrine of negative interest, thereby anticipating Jhering. Windscheid refers to Savigny, *System*, iii, sec. 138, n. 1d. An examination of this passage shows that Savigny would allow compensation only in case the damage was caused by *dolus*, and that he expressly denies the declarant's liability for *culpa*.

was not commercially capable of being sold. Thus, a sale of a burial plot, which was a *res religiosa,* was absolutely void. The object was *extra commercium,* and performance was, therefore, impossible. Modestinus held that "although the purchase does not hold, yet the purchaser will have an action on the purchase against the vendor to recover damages for being misled." [1]

From the duty to use care in contracting, Jhering inferred that the party who failed to discharge this duty was guilty of negligence. Hence, he entitled the article in which his theory was first presented, "Culpa in contrahendo." He based liability for negative damages on negligence. Where he could not find actual negligence, he depended on a presumption of negligence. In one passage he suggested the theory of an implied warranty, which in some respects would seem to present a more satisfactory basis of liability. This implied warranty is simply that the party is able to conclude the particular contract and that it will be valid after it is concluded. The advantage, however, of basing the declarant's liability on laches (*culpa in contrahendo*) consists in the recovery of damages upon the basis of the original contract, which though void for every other purpose, is preserved for this one. When the theory of warranty is involved, the recovery is purely on the warranty and not on the contract.

As already intimated, full recognition has been accorded to Jhering's doctrine in the German civil code. Thus, if a declaration is annulled, according to the provisions of sections 119 and 120, the declarant must make compensation, in case the declaration was addressed to a particular person, to such person, and in other cases to every third person, for the damage which such person suffers by reason of his reli-

[1] Dig. 18, 1, 62, § 1. *Cf.* Munroe Smith, *op. cit.*, p. 45.

ance on the validity of such declaration, but not beyond the amount of the interest which such person has in the validity of the declaration. The duty to make compensation does not arise when the other party knew the ground of nullity, or failed to know it because of his negligence.[1] Again, in section 142, which treats of the retroactive effect of annulment, it is stated that any person who knew or was bound to know that the act was assailable (*anfechtbar*) is treated as if he knew or was bound to know that it was null.[2]

The doctrine of negative interest has found almost universal acceptance among German jurists. Thus, Dernburg holds that, at modern Roman law, if one makes an offer in a negligent manner, and thereby causes another person to conclude what he had reason to believe was a valid contract, the party who made the offer is bound to put such other party in the same position which he would have occupied in case there had been no offer.[3] Under the Prussian law, also, as he points out, negative damages can be awarded whenever the declarant's mistake was due to actual negligence on his part.[4]

Windscheid also recognizes the doctrine of negative interest, but rejects the theory that it is based on negligence. In the earlier editions of his *Pandekten* he based the liability of the declarant on "a tacit warranty" (*eine stillschweigende Garantieübernahme*); in the latest edition published during his life he abandons this theory, declaring that "the duty of the author of the declaration to compensate the

[1] *Bürgerliches Gesetzbuch*, sec. 122.

[2] For further applications of the doctrine of negative interest, which are outside of the limits of this paper, see Munroe Smith, *loc. cit.*

[3] Dernburg, *Pandekten*, ii, p. 27.

[4] Dernburg, *Preussisches Privatrecht*, i, p. 231, ii, p. 39.

other party is not based on his will; the law imposes it on him without regard to his will." [1] Goldschmidt holds that if a contract is void for mistake, the party must be held answerable for his declaration at least in so far as is compatible with the nullity of the contract.[2]

Röver, however, criticizes the doctrine of negative interest, because it is very indefinite, and because it is far better to avoid any damage in the first place than to compensate it afterward.[3] This argument naturally flows from Röver's objective theory of contract. Bähr is forced to take the same position, holding that the problem which Jhering set for himself can be solved in a better way by taking the contract as it stands.[4] To assume a warranty that there is a valid contract, is simply to say that the mistaken party must let the contract operate at least to the extent of binding himself.[5] Bähr, however, in making this assertion, shows that he does not fully understand Jhering's position, for Jhering's avowed object was to prevent an invalid contract from operating as if it were valid.

The right to compensation, though not the theory of negative interest in contract, was recognized in the old Prussian *Landrecht*.[6] And the Austrian civil code as well as the Saxon accords compensation for damage flowing from the nullity of contracts.[7] In fact, it was the provisions of the older codes which first presented to Jhering the idea of a negative interest in contracts to be protected as such.

[1] Windscheid, *Pandekten* (7th ed.), ii, sec. 307, n. 5.

[2] Goldschmidt, *Handelsrecht*, p. 548, n. 11.

[3] Röver, *Ueber die Bedeutung des Willens bei Willenserklärungen*, pp. 9, 13.

[4] Bähr, "Ueber Irrungen im Contrahiren" in *Jahrbücher für die Dogmatik*, xiv, pp. 396–400.

[5] *Ibid.*, xiv, pp. 419–424.

[6] *Allgemeines Landrecht*, I, iv, secs. 56, 79; II, v, secs. 53, 284, 285.

[7] *Oesterreichisches Gesetzbuch*, sec. 878. *Sächsisches Gesetzbuch*, sec. 844.

PART III

ANGLO-AMERICAN LAW

CHAPTER I

THE LIMITATIONS OF THE SUBJECT

IN order to secure a clear treatment of the subject in hand, which is mistake in contract, operating to conceal a variation between intent and declaration and resulting in nullity, certain other connected or related topics must be eliminated. The matter of mistake in motive must be excluded, as must also the subordinate special topics of fraud, unjust enrichment, testamentary dispositions and gifts *mortis causa,* because the juristic acts which receive variant treatment in these branches of the law are founded upon actual consent, and are, therefore, not void but merely voidable because of mistake in motive. Other topics which should be excluded are *dissensus,* impossibility of performance, and failure of conditions precedent. Each of these last-mentioned topics may involve, to a greater or less degree, the consideration of mistake, but their inclusion has tended, even more than the inclusion of the topics first mentioned, to confuse the treatment of the subject here under consideration, because they present closer analogies to this subject. When the declarations do not agree, when performance is objectively impossible, and when a condition precedent fails, the act is as completely devoid of legal result as in the case of essential variations between will and declaration. The fundamental distinction is that, in the case of *dissensus*, impossibility of performance and failure of condition precedent, the single juristic act of each party is perfect, while in the cases which we have to consider the juristic act of one or both parties is defective. Moreover, in the cases of impossibility of performance and of failure of conditions precedent mistake is not invariably present. The failure to observe this distinction has led writers not only to confuse the two classes, but to assign mistake as a ground of relief in both alike.

When a *dissensus* occurs, each party to the supposed contract has actually willed his declaration and has produced, as far as he is concerned, a juristic act. The reason why there is no contract is that the juristic acts do not correspond to each other; the results aimed at are not identical. In mathematical language we should say that the conditions of an equation are wanting. Such cases ought clearly to be excluded from the subject of mistake as here treated. Although there is a mistake by each party as to the nature or content of the juristic act produced by the other party, yet the ground of relief is not mistake, but the absence of that indispensable contractual element which has been immemorially termed the agreement of the wills or the meeting of the minds.

In Turner *v.* Webster,[1] the plaintiff agreed to act as watchman in a factory, which was then under the control of the court, "for $1.50 a day, and nights the same," meaning thereby to separate the day into two parts. The defendant understood the offer to be for both day and night at the rate of $1.50 for twenty-four hours. The court decided that there was no contract, for there was a pure *dis-*

[1] 24 Kansas, 38.

sensus. The plaintiff was permitted to recover on a *quantum meruit* for the value of his services. So also in Kyle *v.* Kavanagh,[1] the court said that "if the defendant was negotiating for one thing, and the plaintiff was selling another thing, and their minds did not agree as to the subject-matter of the sale, there would be no contract by which the defendant would be bound, although there was no fraud on the part of the plaintiff."

The case of Raffles *v.* Wichelhaus [2] has always been cited without any real reason as an instance of mistake, and has, therefore, been the innocent cause of considerable confusion. The real issue in any case must necessarily be ascertained from the pleadings. Fortunately, the report of this case states the essence of the pleadings. The plaintiff brought suit in the month of January against the defendant for not accepting delivery of a cargo of cotton to arrive *ex* steamer "Peerless" from Bombay. The defendant pleaded that he meant to accept delivery from a steamer "Peerless" which was to sail from Bombay during the following October, and that the plaintiff was not ready to deliver from that particular ship, but was ready to deliver from another ship "Peerless" which had sailed from Bombay during the previous December. The court held that the defense was good, and that there had been no meeting of the minds.

In Thornton *v.* Kempster,[3] a broker was employed by both parties to the action as their common representative in a transaction involving the sale and purchase of hemp. By mistake the broker delivered to the vendor a sold-note of Petersburgh hemp, while he delivered to the vendee a bought-note of Riga Rhine hemp. The court insisted upon treating the case as though there had been no broker, and as though the notes were directly exchanged as stated. The decision was that

[1] 103 Mass., 356. [2] 2 H. & C., 906. [3] 5 Taunt., 786.

the contract must be on the one side to sell, and on the other side to accept, one and the same thing. The parties, so far as appeared, had never agreed that the one should sell and the other accept the same thing; consequently there was no agreement subsisting between them.

In Barton *v.* Capron,[1] an auctioneer put up and sold a box as lot number 25. A purchaser bid it in, thinking it was another box, namely, that described in the catalogue as number 24. The court held that neither lot was sold, and that the titles remained unchanged. "No contract was made. The plaintiffs were selling one thing and the defendant was purchasing, or rather bidding upon, another."

All of the foregoing cases clearly belong to the same category of *dissensus*. Their treatment is exceedingly simple. The ground of nullity is simply the failure of the minds to meet. The mistake consists in the erroneous belief that they did meet. It is not the mistake, but the *dissensus*, which makes these contracts void.

When performance of a contract is impossible, this fact may be a sufficient ground of nullity. Each party has produced a juristic act, and the acts aim at an identical result. The mistake relates entirely to the possibility of attaining the result. As a general rule, impossibility of performance is not a ground of nullity, for every one has a right to contract as he pleases. To hold that impossibility of performance is always a ground of nullity would in many cases deprive an injured party of damages to which he is fairly entitled. But if performance was impossible from the beginning, and this fact was unknown to the parties at the inception of the contract, or if performance becomes impossible through *vis major*, it may be said that the parties contracted with reference to the possibility of performance.

[1] 3 R. I., 171.

In this sense possibility of performance is analogous to a condition precedent.

On whatever ground the nullity be explained, it is clear that the mistake is not the dominant factor.

Common illustrations of impossibility of performance are the cases of the sale of a house already destroyed by fire, or the sale of a plantation in a distant country, which had been destroyed the day before by a tornado. In both instances the contract is still capable of enforcement, but the performance in the manner intended has become impossible. In the case of Taylor *v.* Caldwell,[1] the defendant contracted to rent a music-hall for certain days, and in the meantime the hall was destroyed by fire. The court refused to enforce the contract for rent, on the ground of impossibility of performance, and treated the case as being analogous to a condition precedent.

When a condition is made the turning-point upon which the validity of a contract depends, it is easy to see that its failure is the real ground of nullity. Both parties may have produced perfect juristic acts, and these in turn may be directed to an identical result, yet nullity may ensue because of the condition precedent. There are many cases, the decision of which rests upon the assumption of a condition precedent, which might equally well have been decided in the same manner because of impossibility of performance. Thus in Strickland *v.* Turner [2] an annuity, which had been assigned to trustees with power to sell, was sold to the plaintiff a few days after the death of the annuitant. The plaintiff recovered back his money on the common counts, but the case stands for something more than an unjust enrichment. It may well be sustained on the ground of impossibility of performance. It may also be sustained on the

[1] 3 B. & S., 824. [2] 7 Ex. Rep., 206.

ground of an implied condition precedent, for the plaintiff had a right to assume that the annuitant was alive, and the trustees were bound to know that the plaintiff purchased on this assumption. If the trustees had been the plaintiffs, in the position of trying to enforce the sale, the court could not have sustained its actual decision except on the theory of a condition precedent or on that of impossibility of performance.

An analogous case is that of Couturier *v.* Hastie,[1] in which it appeared that the plaintiffs were merchants at Smyrna, and the defendant was a *del credere* corn factor at London, who sold the plaintiffs' corn to a purchaser. Both parties thought that the corn was then on board ship bound for London, whereas in fact it had become heated and had been unloaded and sold at Tunis. The purchaser repudiated the sale "on the ground that the cargo did not exist at the date of the contract." The court held "that the contract imported that at the time of the sale the corn was in existence as such, and capable of delivery." The House of Lords, upon appeal, held "that the whole question turns upon the construction of the contract which was entered into between the parties. What the parties contemplated, those who bought and those who sold, was that there was an existing something to be sold and bought." Clearly the language of this decision might import either a condition precedent to the validity of the contract, or that the contract was null because of impossibility of performance.

In Gibson *v.* Pelkie,[2] the plaintiff agreed to collect a certain judgment for half the proceeds. In fact, the judgment was void, and the court held that for want of a subject-matter there was no contract. So also in Bingham *v.* Bingham,[3] the plaintiff by mistake purchased his own land.

[1] 5 H. L. C., 673. [2] 37 Mich., 380. [3] 1 Ves. Sr., 126.

Upon filing a bill to recover back his money, the court held that "there was a plain mistake such as the court was warranted to relieve against." And in Cooper *v.* Phibbs,[1] the plaintiff leased what later was found to be his own fishery. The court both rescinded the lease and declared the title to be in the plaintiff. Such cases as these, although decided on the supposition of a condition precedent, can equally well be decided in the same manner upon the theory of impossibility of performance.

Cochrane *v.* Willis,[2] however, affords an instance of a condition precedent which cannot be converted into a case of impossibility of performance. This was a bill for specific performance. A tenant in tail expectant upon the death of a life-tenant, who was insolvent, agreed with the assignee that the timber standing on the estate should be considered as belonging to the assignee on a certain day past, provided the assignee would let the timber stand for one month. The life-tenant was in fact dead at the date of this agreement. The court refused relief because there was an assumption at the time that the life-tenant was alive. Performance of this contract was at no time impossible. In cases such as this, the real existence of circumstances supposed by the parties to exist is a condition precedent to the validity of the contract.

All of the foregoing cases are liable to cause confusion, because of the fact that the contract is null, just as in the cases where mistake conceals a variation between will and declaration. In each of them, it must be noted, the juristic act of each party accurately expresses his real intention. Nullity results because of a want of *consensus* between the two parties, or because of impossibility of performance, or because some condition precedent has not been fulfilled.

[1] L. R., 2 H. L., 149. [2] 1 Ch. App., 58.

The mistake is either as to the meaning of the declaration of the other party, or as to possibility of performance, or as to the existence of some person or subject-matter. The exclusion of these cases is necessary in a clear treatment of our main theme, which has to do with invalidity of contract only when the invalidity results from a defect in the juristic act of one party and when such defect is occasioned by mistake.

CHAPTER II

Theories and Opinions

In European continental countries, and especially in Germany, a commentary on the law is something quite different from an English or American treatise. To judicial decisions as such the European legal writer attributes no conclusive authority. He recognizes that the persistent practice of the courts may become law by force of custom, but until such a persistent practice is established—and for this a very long time seems to be regarded as necessary—he regards the decisions of even the highest courts simply as arguments. The opinions of previous writers of recognized reputation are to him quite as important as judicial decisions, and as against both he retains the freedom of his own opinion. The attitude of the courts themselves is theoretically the same, and the opinion of a Pothier, a Savigny, a Windscheid or a Jhering may prevail with them over their own previous decisions.

Very different conditions prevail in the countries living under English law. Every writer of law books has for his first object to state the law as he is able to gather it from the actual decisions. If he disagrees with the cases, his opinion does not have the effect even of a judicial *dictum*. The courts decide a case upon the authority or analogy of existing cases. Writers are, indeed, referred to in the reports, but it is only by way of corroboration, or when the cases seem to be in conflict, or in support of some new principle which the court feels impelled to lay down for the first time. When a principle is laid down for the first time, the case becomes a leading one, but the jurist who was responsible for it and to whom the credit is due is seldom mentioned, nor is his service to legal science long remembered. For this reason the legal literature upon such a subject as the present is extremely limited, if we omit the opinions found in the reported cases.

Holland, who stands for the objective theory, urges that "an investigation into the correspondence between the inner will and its outward manifestations is in most cases impossible, and where possible, is in many cases undesirable." [1] Again, he says that

> there is something to be said for the view, maintained by a recent school of writers, that, in enumerating the requisites of a valid juristic act, we may leave out of account the inscrutable will, and look solely to what purports to be its outward expression. We shall hope later to establish that this is at all events the case with that species of juristic act which is called a contract.[2]

He questions the theory that a contract requires a *consensus,* or a meeting of the minds, and is inclined to hold that "the law looks, not at the will itself, but at the will as voluntarily manifested." He admits that the weight of authority is against him, but insists that the prevailing doctrine is gradually being displaced by the objective theory. He supports himself entirely upon those cases which involve a mistake as to the content of the act, and his argument with reference to this class of cases cannot well be refuted. But when he insists that the objective theory of contract is also consistent with the doctrine of "essential error in prevent-

[1] Holland, *Elements of Jurisprudence*, pp. 112, 113.

[2] *Ibid.*, pp. 114, 115.

ing a contract from coming into existence," his argument is hardly convincing. He says:

Even here the failure of the contract is due not to the psychological fact of mistaken belief, which, as has been well observed, is a mere "dramatic circumstance," [1] but to other causes, which may be reduced to two. (1) The language employed is such as under the circumstance is meaningless, either from reference to an object not in existence, as in the case of the sale of a cargo of corn, supposed to be on its homeward voyage while in reality it had become so heated that it had been unloaded and sold; [2] or from ambiguity, as in the case of the sale of a cargo of cotton "to arrive *ex* 'Peerless' from Bombay," whereas there were two ships, either of which would have answered the description.[3] (2) The true meaning of the mistaken party is, or might be, known to the other party. This will cover the cases of *error in persona, in corpore, in negotio, etc.*, as, for instance, the case where a customer sent an order for goods to a tradesman with whom he had been accustomed to deal, but who had disposed of his business to a successor, who, having supplied the goods without any notification of the change, was not allowed to recover their price.[4] The question in these cases should always be: was the expression of one party such as should fairly have induced the other to act upon it? If so, but not otherwise, it is in the interest of society that the loss should fall upon the former.[5]

The cases cited under Holland's first class are either cases of *dissensus* or of impossibility of performance. The reasons for excluding these cases have been stated above. In the

[1] Holmes, *Common Law*, p. 308. [Holland's citation.]

[2] Couturier *v.* Hastie, 5 H. L. C., 673. [Holland's citation.]

[3] Raffles *v.* Wichelhaus, 2 H. & C., 906. [Holland's citation.]

[4] Boulton *v.* Jones, 2 H. & N., 564. Boston Ice Co. *v.* Potter, 123 Mass., 28. [Holland's citations.]

[5] Holland, *Elements of Jurisprudence*, pp. 251, 252.

cases included in his second class, Holland takes the position that if the mistake is not known to the other party, nullity will not follow.[1] This position, however, as will appear later, is not sustained by the decisions of the courts.

Anson agrees in substance with Holland, but criticizes his statement of the theory:

Professor Holland . . . holds that the law does not ask for "a union of wills" but only for the phenomena of such a union. I hold that the law does require the wills of the parties to be at one, but that when men present all the phenomena of agreement they are not allowed to say that they were not agreed. For all practical purposes our conflict of view is immaterial.[2]

He asserts in another passage that

the cases [in which mistake will vitiate an agreement] are exceptions to an almost universal rule that a man is bound by an agreement to which he has expressed his assent in unequivocal terms, uninfluenced by falsehood, violence, or oppression. If he has exhibited all the outward signs of agreement the law will hold that he has agreed.[3]

In stating these exceptions he follows the customary classification; but he remarks that mistake as to the nature of the transaction arises almost of necessity from misrepresentation, and he narrows the field of mistake as to the subject-matter by treating many of the cases usually brought under this head as cases of failure of performance.[4]

Kerr fails clearly to separate mistake from fraud and mis-

[1] Holland's rule in this class of cases is clearly derived from Leonhard. See Holland, *op. cit.*, p. 252, note 1.

[2] Anson, *Principles of the English Law of Contract* (5th ed., 1888), p. 9, note.

[3] *Ibid.*, p. 125. [4] *Ibid.*, pp. 125-138.

representation.[1] He supports the objective theory of contract, being influenced by Freeman *v.* Cooke,[2] Smith *v.* Hughes,[3] and similar cases.[4] The cases treated by him deal only with relief in equity, or presume a condition precedent. Those cases which cannot be explained in this way, such as Thorogood's case [5] and Foster *v.* Mackinnon,[6] appear to be completely ignored. Kerr seems to accept the doctrine of Smith *v.* Hughes, just cited, as the general principle, and apparently regards all relief for mistake as exceptional. He misrepresents Savigny in holding that the latter made nullity of a contract for mistake dependent upon the question of excusability or absence of negligence.

Pollock is the most satisfactory of the English writers in his treatment of the subject of mistake. He is confessedly influenced by Savigny, whose views he adopts to a certain extent, paying to him the compliment of having cleared up the confusion which existed at both the civil and common law upon this subject.[7] Pollock insists that "mistake does not of itself affect the validity of contracts at all. But mistake may be such as to prevent any real agreement from being formed; in which case the agreement is void." [8] This class of mistake he terms "fundamental error," in order to mark the "broad distinction in principle from those cases where mistake appears as a ground of special relief." This class, of course, corresponds with Savigny's *unecht* class. Pollock further subdivides this class, as does Savigny, into mistake as to the nature of the transaction, as to the person of the other party, and as to the subject-matter of the agreement.[9] He draws, however, a broader distinction of his

[1] Kerr, *Fraud and Mistake*, 2 ed., pp. 470–476.
[2] 2 Ex., 654. [3] L. R., 6 Q. B., 597.
[4] Kerr, *op. cit.*, p. 486. [5] 2 Co. Rep., 9. [6] L. R., 4 C. P., 711.
[7] Pollock, *Contracts* (4th ed.), p. 393. [8] *Ibid.*, p. 392.
[9] *Ibid.*, pp. 412 *et seq.*

own between cases where the "minds never met" and cases where "there does exist a common intention, which, however, is founded on an assumption made by both parties as to some matter of fact essential to the agreement." In these latter cases, also, the mistake is fatal to the existence of an agreement, but the mistake must be common to both parties.[1]

Leake's treatment of mistake is valuable.[2] In his opinion, mistake may affect the act of agreement itself, or its content, or its application, or some "collateral fact or circumstance that is material in inducing the agreement." His first two classes correspond to those distinguished by Pollock. The third class is unsatisfactory; it includes cases which properly belong under *dissensus*, impossibility of performance or conditions precedent. They are not cases of divergence between will and declaration. The fourth class corresponds to mistake in motive, but also includes conditions precedent. Leake's treatment of the first and second classes is admirable.

Although the scope of Fry's treatise on *Specific Performance* excludes consideration of the important cases decided at common law, as distinguished from equity, he states the true doctrine very clearly. He asserts that

> a mistake may be of such a character as, in the view of a purely common law court, to avoid the contract on the ground of want of consent. But equity requires still more than that the contract should be merely legal. It must not be hard, *etc.*, or due to mistake, for there is not that consent which is essential to a contract in equity.[3]

Specific performance, he holds, ought not to be granted against a defendant pleading mistake, although he is in-

[1] Pollock, *Contracts* (4th ed.), pp. 411, 412.

[2] Leake, *Law of Contract*, pp. 311 *et seq.*

[3] Fry, *Specific Performance*. p, 361.

clined to qualify this rule when the defendant appears to have been negligent.[1]

Benjamin states that

> when the mistake is that of one party alone, it must be borne in mind that the general rule of law is that, whatever a man's real intention may be, if he manifests an intention to another party so as to induce the latter to act upon it in making a contract, he will be estopped from denying that the intention as manifested was his real intention.[2]

This assertion being made with reference to sales, is quite correct; but the cases on which it is based relate, as will be shown hereafter, only to mistakes as to the content of the declaration.

Wharton presents a clear statement of the German theories. While he favors the reaction toward the objective theory of contract, he admits the decided preponderance of the subjective theory even in the English law. Thus he says:

> In our own law, the same rule is now generally recognized. Undoubtedly there are many cases of apparent conflict as to details. But on the general question, there is almost an unbroken line of authority, to the effect that there is no contract when the parties have in mind essentially different things. A party may be estopped from denying what he said; but unless this be the case, and this is only so when it is equitable [that] he should be so estopped, he is not contractually bound to something essentially different from what he had in mind.[3]

Wharton excludes those cases of so-called mistake which are in reality cases of impossibility of performance.[4]

[1] Fry, *Specific Performance*, p. 367. [2] Benjamin, *Sales*, p. 62.

[3] Wharton, *Contracts*, vol. i, sec. 178, p. 251.

[4] *Ibid.*, pp. 251, 252; and secs. 296 *et seq.*, pp. 438 *et seq.*.

CHAPTER III

Mistake as to the Act

Nothing can be more conclusive than the evidence which exists in English and American decisions to prove that an act which is not accompanied by a corresponding will or intention is void. A contract is a juristic act expressed in the form of an equation; it is composed of two acts intended to effect a single result. Consequently, the same method of treatment may and should be applied to a contract which is employed in determining the validity of the unilateral juristic act. If one of the component acts is null because there is no corresponding will behind it, then the contract itself is also necessarily null. This is merely another way of stating the Roman-German doctrine. German jurisprudence, however, treats mistake regarding the content of the act as a ground of nullity. This is not true in the English law. The following cases deal with mistake as to the act itself. Mistake as to the content of the act will be treated in the following chapter.

In Thorogood's case,[1] the defendant produced in evidence a deed signed by the plaintiff. The evidence showed that the plaintiff was illiterate and signed the deed upon the representation that it was merely a release of arrears upon an annuity, whereas it was in fact a general release of all claims. It was admitted that the signature was the plaintiff's, and it was left to the jury to decide whether the deed was his. The jury found the negative, as well as the absence of negligence.

[1] 2 Co. Rep., 9.

In Foster *v.* Mackinnon,[1] it appeared that the defendant, who was advanced in years and could not see very well, was fraudulently induced to endorse a bill of exchange upon the representation that it was a mere guarantee. The court charged that

if the endorsement was not the signature of the defendant, or if, being his signature, it was obtained upon a fraudulent representation that it was a guarantee, and the defendant signed it without knowing that it was a bill, and under a belief that it was a guarantee, and if the defendant was not guilty of any negligence in so signing the paper, he was entitled to the verdict.

Upon appeal, this was held a proper charge, and Byles, J., held expressly that, if there be no negligence, such signature

is invalid not merely on the ground of fraud, where fraud exists, but on the ground that the mind of the signer did not accompany the signature; in other words, that he never intended to sign, and therefore in contemplation of law never did sign, the contract to which his name is appended.

And in reply to counsel, who urged that, where the plaintiff proves he is a *bona fide* holder for value, it is immaterial that the signature of the defendant was obtained by fraud, —"That," said Chief Justice Bovill, "is where the defendant intended to put his name to an instrument which was a bill." [2]

Both of the foregoing cases involved fraud; but the court in each instance placed the decision squarely upon the principle that an act which is not supported by a real will or consent is absolutely void, and not merely voidable, as would necessarily be the case if the ground of the decision had been fraud. Pollock, in commenting on both cases, says that the doctrine of Thorogood's case

[1] L. R., 4 C. P., 704; 38 L. J. (C. L.), 310.

[2] 38 L. J. (C. L.), 310, at p. 313.

was expounded and confirmed by the luminous judgment . . . in Foster *v.* Mackinnon. . . . This decision shows clearly that an instrument executed by a man who meant to execute not any such instrument but something of a different kind is in itself a mere nullity, though the person so executing it may perhaps be estopped from disputing it if there be any negligence on his part; and that, notwithstanding the importance constantly attached by the law to the security of *bona fide* holders of negotiable instruments, no exception is in this case made in their favor.[1]

The case of Foster v. Mackinnon was cited, and the doctrine there laid down was accepted in the New York case of Whitney *v.* Snyder.[2] In this case the plaintiff was a *bona fide* holder for value of a promissory note. The defendant offered to show that he was unable to read and that he signed the note on the representation that it was a contract of an entirely different nature. This case was expressly distinguished from the case of a note fraudulently obtained, which the maker intended to make.

In the Alabama case of Nance *v.* Lary,[3] the court decided that where a person writes his name on a blank piece of paper, and another person takes possession of the paper, without authority therefor, and writes a promissory note above the signature, which he negotiates to a third person who is ignorant of the circumstances, the writer of the signature is not liable as the maker of the note to the holder. This is rather an extreme case. It would certainly appear to be negligence for one to write his name in blank on a piece of paper suitable for a promissory note and in the position suitable for a signature.

In the Wisconsin case of Walker *v.* Ebert,[4] the defend-

[1] Pollock, *Contracts*, 413-415.

[2] 2 Lans. 477.

[3] 5 Ala., 370.

[4] 29 Wis., 194.

ant, who was an ignorant immigrant, was induced to sign what he thought was a contract of agency to sell machinery on percentage. It turned out to be a promissory note. The court held that

> the party whose signature to such paper is obtained by fraud as to the character of the paper itself, who is ignorant of such character and has no intention of signing it, and who is guilty of no negligence in affixing his signature or in not ascertaining the character of the instrument, is no more bound by it than if it were a total forgery, the signature included.

In De Camp *v.* Hamma,[1] an Ohio case, the defendant was induced to sign a note thinking it was a non-negotiable contract appointing him agent to sell a corn-harvester. The court held that where the maker was not negligent and did not know the nature of the instrument "there is no more reason why he should be obligated thereby than if his signature had been forged."

In the Michigan case of Wait *v.* Pomeroy,[2] the defendant signed a note with a memorandum annexed as part of it. The memorandum was afterward destroyed without his consent, and the note was then negotiated. The court refused to treat the note in this condition as that of the maker.

In another Michigan case, Gibbs *v.* Linabury,[3] the defendant was induced to sign a promissory note on the representation that it was a duplicate of a contract appointing him agent to sell a patent hayfork. There was no negligence, and the court treated the note precisely like a forgery, not even to be enforced in the hands of a *bona fide* holder for value. The court expressly denied the application of the maxim that, as between two innocent parties,

[1] 29 Ohio St., 467. [2] 20 Mich., 425. [3] 22 Mich., 479.

the loss must fall upon the one whose acts enabled a third party to perpetrate a fraud. This maxim, the court said,

presupposes the assent of the will of the actor. If from any cause the assent of the will is wanting, the result is the same as if the act were done under duress, or by an insane man. The point is that the will does not go with the act.

On the other hand, in the West Virginia case of Bank *v.* Johns,[1] the court deliberately overruled the doctrine of Foster *v.* Mackinnon, and also interpreted the maxim above cited according to its literal meaning. The defendant was induced to sign a negotiable note thinking it was a contract of agency to sell a patent washing-machine. The court held bluntly that

when a purchaser of a negotiable note takes it for value before maturity without notice of any fraud in its execution, unless it was at the time so purchased by him absolutely void, he will recover on such note against the maker, although the maker was induced by fraud to sign it, not intending to sign such note but a paper of an entirely different character; and in such case the question of negligence in the maker forms no legitimate subject of inquiry.

This case stands by itself and cannot be accepted as representative of the law.

The rule against negligence was enforced in all its severity in the New Hampshire case of Bank *v.* Smith.[2] The defendant was very old, his eyesight was poor, he was uneducated and unaccustomed to writing. He was induced to sign a note upon the faith that it was a contract of agency to sell a patent hayfork. It appeared that his daughter was present at the signing, and that he did not ask her assist-

[1] 22 W. Va., 532.

[2] 55 N. H., 593.

ance nor make any effort whatever to look into the nature of the instrument. The court held that it was a "negligent act on the part of the defendant to sign the note without ascertaining whether it was what the payee represented, or something else." The case was, therefore, decided purely on the basis of estoppel because of the defendant's negligence. It was cited in support of the preceding case of Bank *v.* Johns, but the decision in the latter case was not based on defendant's negligence. It depended solely on a misapplication of the "two innocent parties" maxim. The case of Bank *v.* Smith must be regarded as agreeing in principle with that of Foster *v.* Mackinnon.

Foster *v.* Mackinnon is unquestionably recognized as law in New York, as was shown in the case of Whitney *v.* Snyder, cited above. The rule as to negligence is, however, also recognized, and to the same extent as in the New Hampshire case of Bank *v.* Smith. Thus, in Chapman *v.* Rose,[1] the defendant signed a note thinking it was a contract appointing him agent to sell a patent hayfork. The note was signed very carelessly, and the court held that, if a person has an opportunity to ascertain the nature of his act, he is negligent if he relies on the statements of the person with whom he is dealing, and that he must accordingly be held liable to third parties who are *bona fide* holders for value. To avoid liability one must show that he was guilty of no negligence in signing. The court approved of Foster *v.* Mackinnon, and held the defendant liable upon the distinct principle of estoppel for negligence.

The same rule was applied in the Indiana case of Baldwin *v.* Barrows.[2] The defendant signed a note upon the mere representation that it was an order for medicines. He was

[1] 56 N. Y., 137. See also Carey *v.* Miller, 25 Hun, 28, in which Chapman *v.* Rose is cited, and the rule of negligence is clearly defined.

[2] 86 Ind., 351.

able to read. The note was signed in the presence of his wife, but he neither read it nor asked his wife to read it, and signed it upon the representation of the person with whom he was dealing. The court held that "where a man negligently signs a note negotiable by the law merchant, he cannot defend against it in the hands of a *bona fide* holder, and ordinarily one who does sign a note without reading it is guilty of negligence."

The courts of Kansas also observe the rule as to negligence. Thus, in Ort *v.* Fowler,[1] the defendant was induced to act as a fence agent, and signed a note without knowing its nature. He was found to be negligent, and therefore liable. The case is very similar to the West Virginia case of Bank *v.* Johns. The West Virginia case, however, asserts the doctrine that where one of two innocent parties must suffer, he by whose *act* the loss has occurred must bear it. The Kansas case follows the rule that where one of two innocent parties must suffer, he whose *negligence* has made possible the perpetration of the fraud must suffer. The Kansas decision is, consequently, in conformity with the New York rule.

The Illinois case of Puffer *v.* Smith,[2] appears to ignore the question of negligence, and to assert the absolute nullity of a note signed in the belief that it was a contract of agency to sell a cultivator and seeder by one who was illiterate and who relied entirely upon the representations of the other party. The case certainly lends strong support to the will theory.

The Missouri case of Briggs *v.* Ewart[3] also appears largely to absolve the defendant from negligence or responsibility for it. The defendant signed what he thought was an order for a pump. It was dark at the time, and the paper was really a note. The court said that

[1] 31 Kan., 478. [2] 57 Ill., 527. [3] 51 Mo., 245.

if he did not know what he was signing, but acted honestly under the belief that he was signing some other paper, and not the one he really signed, he ought not to be bound by such signature. In the execution of instruments of writing, such as contracts, deeds, *etc.*, the mind must act intelligently, and the instrument must not only be signed, but delivered by the party as and for what he intended it for.

The court also held that the purchaser of negotiable paper was bound to make reasonable inquiry as to its genuineness.

In the Indiana case of Cline *v.* Guthrie,[1] the court left it to the jury to say whether it was negligence for the defendant to sign his name in blank to show how it was spelled. So also in Detwiler *v.* Bish,[2] where it appeared that in a contract of agency to sell a pulverizer and cultivator a note was so cunningly concealed as to defy ordinary examination, the court held that this fact was a good defense, and raised a presumption of absence of negligence.

The Iowa courts follow the correct principle. In Douglass *v.* Matting,[3] the defendant acted entirely upon the representation of the party with whom he was dealing, and the court held that this was fatal negligence. In Hopkins *v.* Insurance Company,[4] the court said, with reference to a defendant who signed without using spectacles and who failed to call for assistance from his son or wife, who were both present, that such conduct should go to the jury. The question was whether he acted "as persons of reasonable and ordinary care would usually do under the circumstances. If he did, he was not negligent." In Fayette Bank *v.* Steffes,[5] the defendant intended to sign the instrument in question but for a smaller amount, and he was held

[1] 42 Ind., 227. [2] 44 Ind., 70. [3] 29 Iowa, 498.
[4] 57 Iowa, 207. [5] 54 Iowa, 214.

because he intended to sign a note, though not of such content.

In the Pennsylvania case of Green *v.* North Buffalo Township,[1] it was held that there was a

> palpable distinction between a defence resting upon facts which are misstated in order to induce a party to enter into a bond, the contents of which he knows, and one resting upon a misrepresentation of the contents of the instrument itself to an illiterate person. In the former case the bond is the obligation of the party who seals it, ... in the latter the instrument is not his deed or bond at all.

The court traced the true principle back to Thorogood's case. In the above decision, the phrase "contents of the instrument" designates its character or nature. The mistake was in the act itself.

Vorley *v.* Cooke [2] was a bill in equity by the assignee of a mortgage. Cooke, the defendant, was induced by his solicitor to execute what he thought was the usual form of covenant to produce title deeds, but which was in fact a mortgage to the solicitor, who then assigned it to the complainant, who foreclosed. It appeared, the court said, that

> there was no such mortgage, and no intention or representation that any mortgage was intended, but on the contrary that it was a deed of an entirely different kind. It cannot be said that Cooke's conduct was careless or rash. He was deceived as any one with the ordinary amount of intelligence and caution would have been deceived, and he is therefore entitled to be relieved.

The bill was accordingly dismissed without costs. On the cross-bill, the mortgage was ordered delivered up to be canceled as void.

[1] 56 Pa. St., 110.

[2] 1 Giff., 230.

In the similar case of Ogilvie *v.* Jeafferson,[1] the plaintiff held a mortgage on a leasehold, and was induced by fraud to convey the legal estate, believing that he was making a lease. The defendant was an innocent purchaser under the fraudulent deed. The bill was filed to declare it void and to rescind. It was held that the deed was wholly void, and that the defendant had acquired no right under it. "The plaintiff might plead either fraud, or *non est factum, i. e.*, that the instrument was not his deed, the consenting mind being wanting in the execution."

In Empson's case,[2] it appeared that Empson agreed with a building society to take land from it with a back purchase-money mortgage for the whole amount. The solicitor of the society drew up, in place of the proper mortgage, a deed reciting that Empson was a member and that he had subscribed for a certain number of shares, and containing covenants to pay dues upon them. In fact, he was not a member and had never subscribed. Two years later the society was wound up and Empson refused to contribute. The court sustained him, because the deed did not and could not operate as his act, for it was not a mortgage, as intended, but something entirely different.

In Schulter's case,[3] a man 115 years of age and entirely blind was induced to make leases for fifty-one years without power of revocation, when he intended to execute them to hold only during the minority of his grandchild. The court held that "the said indentures could not bind the said John Schulter for this that he was blind and like to one who could not read at all."

The foregoing cases illustrate mistake *in negotio*, or as to the nature of the transaction. We find an equally clear line of authority when the mistake is *in persona*. The case

[1] 2 Giff., 353. [2] L. R., 9 Eq., 597. [3] 12 Co. Rep., 90.

of Boulton *v.* Jones [1] has always been considered in England as a leading case to show that a mistake as to the person, when such person constitutes the chief reason for making the offer, is fatal to the validity of the contract. The defendant ordered rubber hose from one from whom he was in the habit of buying such goods, but who, just previous to this order, had sold the business to his manager. The latter furnished the goods to the defendant, who knew nothing of the change. "It is a rule of law," the court said, "that if a person intends to contract with A, B cannot give himself any right under it."

In America the same decision was made in the Massachusetts case of Boston Ice Company *v.* Potter.[2] In this case the defendant was accustomed to buy ice from the plaintiff, but becoming dissatisfied gave his patronage to another party, who was later bought out by the plaintiff without defendant's knowledge. It was held that "a party has a right to select and determine with whom he will contract, and cannot have another person thrust upon him without his consent."

In another very important case, Cundy *v.* Lindsay,[3] the plaintiff, a manufacturer in Ireland, was induced by a certain Alfred Blenkarn, of 37 Wood St., Cheapside, London, to deliver goods which were subsequently sold to the defendant, who was an innocent purchaser. The plaintiff intended to deal and thought he was dealing with W. Blenkiron & Co., a reputable firm of 123 Wood St. The court held that "no contract was made with Blenkarn, that even a temporary property in the goods never passed to him, so that he never had a possessory title which he could transfer to the defendants, who were consequently liable to the plaintiff for the value of the goods."

[1] 2 H. & N., 564. [2] 123 Mass., 28. [3] 3 App. Cases, 459.

In Robson *v.* Drummond,[1] the defendant contracted with one Sharpe for a carriage for five years, not knowing that he had a partner named Robson. At the end of three years Sharpe retired in favor of Robson, who offered to complete the contract, which offer was refused by the defendant. It was held that "the defendant may have been induced to enter into this contract by reason of the personal confidence which he reposed in Sharpe," and that he had an absolute right to refuse to deal with any other person.

In *ex parte* Barnett,[2] a person doing business under the name of Joseph Reed & Sons, who had become bankrupt and who was not yet discharged, ordered some casks of sherry from the plaintiff, who thought the order was from Reed, Brothers & Co., a distinct firm. The assignee claimed title, but the court held that the bankrupt had acquired no property in the goods, and that the trustee must return them.

In the majority of instances a mistake as to the person is immaterial. This is the case in the matter of petty sales. Moreover, even where mistake as to the person might otherwise be pleaded, such right is not infrequently waived, particularly when the credit of the party to whom goods have been delivered is as good as that of the party erroneously supposed to be the purchaser. In the case of sales for cash, the identity of the vendee is regularly immaterial. Where, however, special reasons exist for contracting with a particular person, and where, but for the mistake, the contract apparently would not have been concluded, a mistake as to the identity of the person is always fatal to the validity of the contract.

We have yet to consider the case of mistake *in re*, or as to the identity of the object. In the case of Harvey *v.*

[1] 2 B. & Ad., 303. [2] L. R., 3 Ch. Div., 123.

Harris [1] it appeared that an auctioneer had for sale two grades of damaged flour. One grade was only slightly damaged, and was offered for sale in the original barrels. The other grade was repacked and sold as "dough." Both grades stood in the street outside of the auctioneer's door, and were publicly declared to be different from each other. The first or best lot was sold out entire, as the auctioneer believed, after which the "dough" was offered for sale. The plaintiff, as highest bidder, selected two rows by numbers, as and for "dough." In fact, these rows consisted of first-grade barrels, accidentally misplaced without the knowledge of owner or auctioneer. The court said that

there was a mistake as to the identity of the article sold, and not merely as to its quality, and it is a case within that class where, through mistake, a contract which the parties intended to make fails of effect because they did not in fact agree as to the subject-matter.

In Huthmacher *v.* Harris's Administrators,[2] the defendant bought an upright block of wood with a wheel attachment on top, inventoried as a drill machine. He took it home and split it up, whereupon a secret drawer fell out containing money and jewelry. It was decided that no title had passed and that there was no sale. "The contract of sale, like all other contracts, is to be controlled by the clearly ascertained intention of the parties."

In Malins *v.* Freeman,[3] it appeared that the defendant was employed by one Davies to bid on the latter's property at auction for the purpose of protecting it. The complainant's property was to be sold on the same day by the same auctioneer, but immediately before the sale of the Davies property. The defendant came into the room while lot

[1] 112 Mass., 32. [2] 38 Pa. St., 491. [3] 2 Keen, 25.

number three of the complainant's property was being sold, and, thinking it was the Davies property, bid it in as the highest bidder. The bill was for specific performance, and it was dismissed because of the defendant's mistake, the complainant being left to his remedy at law. It appeared, however, as a fact that the defendant was at once apprised of his mistake, but failed to notify the auctioneer of his position until after the bidding was closed. The court evidently ignored this element of negligence. The case, while sound as far as it goes, would not be approved to-day. Negligence, as will appear in the case of Tamplin *v.* James,[1] to be noticed later, may well overcome whatever equity the defendant may otherwise possess.

The foregoing cases illustrate the subject of mistake in the act itself, and furnish ample proof of the existence of Savigny's doctrine in the English and American law. From them must be distinguished the case of mistake as to the content of the act, when the act itself is willed. In this matter the English and American decisions show a marked divergence from Savigny's doctrine.

[1] L. R., 15 Chan. Div., 215.

CHAPTER IV

Mistake as to the Content of the Act

There is no authority of a legal nature for the proposition that a man is to be judged by his acts and declarations solely, and never by his intentions. On the contrary, the evidence is conclusive that an act which is not willed is, according to the common law, entirely void. The intention to do the act is an indispensable prerequisite to its validity. The evidence is equally conclusive that if an act is willed, then its author is to be judged according to such act, even though its content be contrary to his will or intention. The content of the act, according to which his responsibility is measured, is simply that meaning which a reasonable third person would put upon such act. A man, therefore, may well be bound by his act although he did not will or intend its content, *i. e.*, although he was mistaken in regard to its content. This is the common-law doctrine. The failure to note this distinction has been at the root of much of the confusion which admittedly exists in the discussion of the common-law doctrine of mistake.

The doctrine of the common law has received some recognition in Germany, but the theory of Savigny and the prevailing German doctrine of to-day accord to a mistake as to the content of the act the same treatment which is accorded to a mistake as to the act itself. As the German law is now framed in the imperial code, there is no reason for treating these two classes of mistake differently. Any injustice or hardship which would otherwise result from the absence of differentiation is remedied, possibly not as generously as in the common law, but nevertheless more equitably, by the legislative acceptance of Jhering's doctrine of negative interest.

The reasons for the sharp distinction drawn in the common law between mistake as to the act and mistake as to the content of the act are not difficult to ascertain. No other system of law has elaborated so complex a body of rules regarding evidence; and in no other system is the body of substantive law so often crossed and modified by the law of evidence. Among the English rules of evidence is one of great importance, which bears directly upon the present subject. It is well settled that parol evidence cannot be introduced to alter or vary the terms of a written instrument. Were it affirmed to be a well settled principle of substantive English law that a mistake as to the content of an act is ground for nullity of the contract, it would still be necessary to concede that the principle is practically inapplicable to the case where the expression of the will is in writing. In all such cases the alleged substantive rule would fail because the rule of evidence excludes the facts upon which it should operate; and the contract which is theoretically void because one of the parties intended no act of such a content must be treated precisely as though it were valid.

The doctrine of estoppel, moreover, covers cases in which the original declaration was not embodied in any written instrument. The rule that a man is precluded from denying that his act meant what it seemed to mean is established in two leading cases, which have long been familiar, Freeman *v.* Cooke and Smith *v.* Hughes. The latter case was probably largely influenced by the former.

Freeman *v.* Cooke [1] was an action of trover against the sheriff of Yorkshire, by the assignees of one William Broadbent, for goods of the bankrupt. It appeared that when the sheriff went to levy upon these goods as belonging to Benjamin Broadbent, William admitted that the goods did belong to Benjamin and not to himself. Later he said that they belonged to another brother, and finally he claimed them as his own. The sheriff then seized them. They were in fact the goods of William. As against the assignees, the sheriff pleaded estoppel through the conduct of William in inducing him to believe that the goods were not in the bankrupt's estate. The court admitted the plea to be good on principle, but held that upon the evidence he had not brought himself within the plea, because William, by his later statements, had done enough to put the sheriff under doubt as to who was the real owner. The court laid down the rule as follows:

> If, whatever a man's real intention may be, he so conducts himself that a reasonable man would take the representation to be true, and believe that it was meant that he should act upon it, and did act upon it as true, the party making the representation would be equally precluded from contesting its truth; and conduct, by negligence or omission, when there is a duty cast upon a person, by usage of trade or otherwise, to disclose the truth, may often have the same effect.

This decision, of course, does not establish any direct precedent as regards the effect of mistake; it merely defines the limits of estoppel.

In the case of Smith *v.* Hughes,[2] the plaintiff sold some oats to the defendant, who thought they were old oats, whereas in fact they were new and unsuitable. The question was whether the defendant acted upon his own opinion,

2 Ex., 654.

[2] L. R., 6 Q. B., 597.

or whether the conduct of the plaintiff was such as to induce the defendant to think that the plaintiff was offering old oats and not new ones. The court expressly approved of the rule as laid down in Freeman *v.* Cooke, and decided that if the defendant acted on his own opinion, he was liable, but if he was entitled to believe that the plaintiff represented the oats to be old, the latter would be estopped from denying that he had offered old oats.

The important distinction between mistake in the act itself and mistake in the content of the act, which was touched upon in the case of Whitney *v.* Snyder,[1] has received a fine illustration in the case of McWilliams *v.* Mason.[2] In this latter case the defendant signed a bond, intending to become liable only as guarantor on a negotiable note. The bond was then negotiated to the plaintiff, who was a *bona fide* purchaser for value without notice. It was held that "the law imposes the loss upon the party who by his misplaced confidence has enabled another, on the faith of his obligation, to obtain the money or property of a third person, who has dealt in good faith, relying on such obligation." The important feature in the case consists in the fact that the defendant actually intended to execute the bond. He was mistaken as to the proper content of his act, and discovered, when it was too late, that he was not merely a guarantor but an obligor, bound to answer for his act to every innocent assignee for value.

In Van Duzer *v.* Howe,[3] the defendant accepted three drafts in blank upon the faith of an oral agreement that they were not to be filled out in the aggregate for an amount to exceed one thousand dollars. The maker forthwith filled out one of them for twelve hundred dollars, and negotiated it to the plaintiff who was an innocent purchaser for value.

[1] 2 Lans., 477. [2] 31 N. Y., 294. [3] 21 N. Y., 531.

It was held that the defendant was liable. As between the original parties the act was voidable, but "binding as between the public and the person giving the blank acceptance."

The case of Abbott *v.* Rose[1] needs to be carefully distinguished from superficially similar cases noticed in the preceding chapter. The defendant signed a note in blank during negotiations looking toward his appointment as agent to sell a machine to "load hay and manure, dig potatoes and ditch." He was "rushed" into signing the paper and admitted his foolishness. He was held liable to a *bona fide* purchaser for value who brought suit. The point to be noted in the case is that he intended to sign a note, *i. e.*, the very kind of paper which he did sign, although he did not intend to assume the obligations which his signature entailed upon him. If he had intended to execute an instrument of an entirely different nature, the note would not have been his act at all and he would not have been liable.

In the Massachusetts case of Putnam *v.* Sullivan,[2] blank notes were intrusted to a clerk, who filled out and negotiated three of them contrary to his instructions. The court applied the rule that where one of two innocent parties must suffer, he must bear the loss whose negligence enabled the fraud to be perpetrated.

In an Iowa case, Fayette Bank *v.* Steffes,[3] it appeared that the defendant intended to sign a note for a lesser sum than was actually named. There was no one within two miles who could translate the note into the defendant's language. The court said that "a sharp distinction is made between such a case and one where the maker supposed that he was executing an instrument not a note." If one intends to execute a note, "he must know that he is furnishing means whereby third parties may be affected."

[1] 62 Me., 194. [2] 4 Mass., 45. [3] 54 Ia., 214.

An important New York case is that of Phillip *v.* Gallant.[1] The defendant executed a building contract which she understood to include an obligation on the part of the plaintiff to complete work of a former contractor. In fact there was no provision of this sort in the contract, and the plaintiff knew nothing about the defendant's belief in the matter. The court proceeded directly upon the authority of Smith *v.* Hughes,[2] holding the defendant strictly to her contract as expressed. It added that

> the general rule that a party is not bound by the terms of a contract which he does not assent to is well established, but under circumstances like those developed in this case the party is bound, because he is deemed to have assented to the terms, and also because he has so acted as to induce the other party to enter into the contract and is therefore precluded from asserting that he did not assent.

The defendant had a clear intention to execute the contract, but was mistaken as to its terms or content.

In Hotson *v.* Browne,[3] the defendant was induced by an advertising agent to send to the plaintiff his written order for insertions in the plaintiff's publications, the "charge for insertion to be ten shillings in each monthly book." The defendant in some way thought this price was the total for all the insertions, and upon trial attempted to prove what had passed between him and the agent. The court held that, in the absence of allegations of fraud, such evidence was inadmissible, because it conflicted with the rule against parol evidence to vary a written instrument. The defendant's mistake was consequently without remedy.

In Stoddard *v.* Ham [4] we have a case which might well cause some perplexity. The plaintiff sold some bricks to

[1] 62 N. Y., 256.
[2] L. R., 6 Q. B., 597.
[3] 9 C. B., N. S., 441.
[4] 129 Mass., 383.

one Leonard, who was a commission merchant as well as an independent dealer. The plaintiff thought that Leonard was buying as agent for the defendant, to whom Leonard subsequently in fact sold the bricks. It appeared, however, that the plaintiff did not disclose his belief that Leonard was an agent, but dealt with him to all appearances as principal. The court held that Boston Ice Co. *v.* Potter [1] was not applicable. Here was an unrevealed intention contrary to what was apparently indicated. Smith *v.* Hughes was not referred to, but the decision was in accordance with the rule there laid down. This case can and should be distinguished from the cases of mistake as to the person noticed in the preceding chapter. The plaintiff intended to deal with Leonard, although he erroneously believed that the sale would operate to bind a third party. He was mistaken not as to the person, but as to the character in which the person was acting.

We have yet to consider the subject of mistake in the content of the act from the standpoint of equity. The cases bearing upon this aspect of the subject present apparent anomalies. These, however, can be satisfactorily explained. Nothing could be more destructive of sound legal reasoning than to hold that there is one basis of contract in law and another in equity. A contract is precisely the same legal entity in equity that it is in law. It must always be kept clearly in mind that when a principle of law or rule of estoppel is laid down, such as was enunciated in Freeman *v.* Cooke [2] and Smith *v.* Hughes, [3] a party who comes within such principle or rule cannot apply to a court of equity in order to obtain what the law itself denies. The cases in equity which bear upon the present aspect of the subject must be explained according to these premises or not at all.

[1] 123 Mass., 28. [2] 2 Ex., 654. [3] L. R., 6 Q. B., 597.

If the mistaken party be made defendant to a bill for specific performance and raise the defense of mistake, all that equity can do is to dismiss the bill and send the parties to law. To do more for the mistaken party would be to concede what the law denies. So much, however, equity does unless he has been guilty of negligence. If the mistaken party seeks to rescind, rescission will not be granted simply because of mistake as to the content of act. But if the mistake was known to the other party, this fact gives the mistaken party an equitable claim to be restored to his former position, because it is unjust that an antagonist should take advantage of what he knows to have been a mistake—of a declaration to which, as he knows, real consent was lacking. Finally, if the written instrument does not represent the real agreement which was entered into, the mistaken party has an equitable claim for reformation, so as to make the apparent agreement conform to the real agreement.

Mansfield *v.* Sherman [1] is an excellent case in specific performance. The defendant, who lived in New York City, owned some lots in Bar Harbor, Maine. He sold one, through mistake as to its exact location, for a price far less than he intended to demand for that precise lot. The court refused specific performance, and left the parties to their remedies at law. The court said:

Not every party who would be entitled as of right to damages for the breach of a contract is entitled to a decree for its specific performance. Before granting such a decree, the court should be satisfied not only of the existence of a valid contract free from fraud and enforceable at law, but also of its fairness and its harmony with equity and good conscience. However strong, clear and emphatic the language of the contract, however plain the right at law, if a specific performance would for any reason

[1] 81 Me., 365.

cause a result harsh, inequitable or contrary to good conscience, the court should refuse such a decree and leave the parties to their remedies at law.

This principle was applied in Leslie *v.* Tompson,[1] where the vendor sold by auction land in plots, and made a mistake in computation of those sold to the complainant. The latter saw that the mistake conduced to his advantage and forthwith filed a bill for specific performance, which was refused.

In Webster *v.* Cecil,[2] the defendant by letter offered to sell his property for 1100 pounds. He meant 2100 pounds, and made the mistake through inadvertence and haste to catch the mail. The complainant desired specific performance. The Master of the Rolls, Sir John Romilly, said that, "in the state of the case, the court could not grant specific performance, and compel a person to sell property for much less than its real value, and for 1000 pounds less than he intended. The complainant might bring such action at law as he might be advised."

In Baxendale *v.* Seale,[3] also before the Master of the Rolls, it appeared that a vendor had agreed to sell a manor which was believed by both parties to be coextensive with a given parish. In fact, the manor extended beyond the parish and included valuable pieces of waste land, besides an important mud bank. The complainant filed a bill for specific performance, insisting that it was a sale and purchase of an uncertain thing. The defendant, however, proved by a preponderance of evidence that his intention was to sell only a manor which did not extend beyond the parish. The court held that the complainant's construction of the contract would unquestionably compel the defendant "to include in the conveyance property not intended or be-

[1] 9 Hare, 268. [2] 30 Beav., 62. [3] 19 Beav., 601.

lieved by him to come within the terms of the contract." The bill was, therefore, properly dismissed.

In Buckhalter *v.* Jones,[1] the defendant in writing accepted complainant's offer in writing to purchase defendant's property for $2000. The defendant, in some inexplicable way, read the offer as though it were for $2100. The court expressly held the contract valid at law; but because of the mistake, which was clearly proved, it refused to grant specific performance, and left the complainant to his remedy at law.

Tamplin *v.* James [2] was a comparatively recent case, and may be accepted as settling the rule of negligence whenever mistake is pleaded as a defense to a bill for specific performance. It appeared that the complainant had sold to the defendant an inn and outbuildings, together with an adjoining saddler's shop. At the rear of each was a small garden not belonging to them, but merely annexed as a convenience. The defendant was perfectly familiar with the properties, but bought in the belief that the annexed gardens went with the main property. As a fact, however, the gardens were expressly excluded. The properties were accurately described according to the public tithe-map, and both map and description were in plain view before the purchaser. The defendant might easily have seen at once that the gardens were excluded had he taken the trouble to read either the map or description, which he deliberately neglected to do. It was held that

> if a man will not take reasonable care to ascertain what he is buying, he must take the consequences. . . . It would open the door to fraud if such a defense were to be allowed. . . . If a man makes a mistake of this kind without any reasonable excuse, he ought to be held to his bargain.

[1] 32 Kan., 5.

[2] 1 Ves. Sr., 457.

This was the universal sentiment of the whole court. The case is not in conflict with those previously noticed. It turns entirely upon the question of negligence, which overcomes whatever equity the defendant may have.

Alvanley *v.* Kinnaird [1] is a very interesting case, both as regards specific performance and rescission. Land belonging to the complainant, in which he intended to reserve all minerals, was sold by mistake without any such reservation. The vendee knew nothing of the mistake. It was intimated that if a bill for specific performance had been filed, it would have been dismissed and the parties left to their remedies at law. The vendor, however, was the complainant, and he filed a bill for either reformation or rescission. The court refused to rescind. It also intimated that the purchaser could not be compelled to complete his purchase excluding the mines; *i. e.*, the contract could not be reformed against his will, evidently because there was no agreement to which it could be made to conform. There was, in fact, no agreement whatever except the contract. As, however, the purchaser was willing to take the lot at the price offered with an express exclusion of the mines, it was ordered that the conveyance be settled accordingly.

In Baker *v.* Paine [2] there were minutes of an agreement concerning a sale of China ware and merchandise brought home by a sea captain. A formal contract was drawn up which contained a covenant not contained in the minutes. Lord Hardwicke asked:

How can a mistake in an agreement be proved but by parol evidence? It is not read to contradict the face of the agreement, which the court would not allow, but to prove a mistake therein, which cannot otherwise be proved . . . . These minutes must be taken to be the agreement of the parties; and if

[1] 2 Mac. & G., 1.

[2] 1 Ves. Sr., 457.

[there be] any material variation (as is admitted for defendant) the articles must be rectified. The question then is, what is the true sense of the minutes?

This case is an excellent illustration of a mistake in content, resulting in a displacement of the actual agreement. Here there was an actual agreement to which to conform.

In Gillespie *v.* Moore [1] a trustee sold 200 acres, and by mistake gave a deed for a larger tract of 250 acres. The defendant stated that he proposed to take advantage of the mistake, and improved the other 50 acres by the erection of a building. The trustee died, but the *cestui* lost no time in filing a bill for relief. The court decreed a reconveyance of the 50 acres without compensation for improvements. The bill was in the nature of a bill for rescission and reformation. There was no question as to the existence of the original agreement.

The complainant in Paget *v.* Marshall [2] owned certain houses, all of which he desired to lease, with the exception of the first floor of one, which he intended to reserve for his own use, and which was so arranged that no one who saw it could fail to perceive the intent and object of the owner. The defendant had personally inspected the premises and verbally noted or remarked the arrangement in question. The complainant offered to lease the whole to the defendant for 500 pounds *per annum*, and upon acceptance the lease was so executed. The bill was filed for rescission. The court, upon the strength of these facts, decreed a rescission of the contract, but gave the defendant the alternative of voluntarily consenting to a reformation in accordance with the original intention of the complainant.

In Loss *v.* Obry,[3] a guardian sold to the defendant one-

[1] 2 John. Ch., 585. [2] 28 Ch. Div., 255. [3] 22 N. J. Eq., 52

fifth of certain land, and by mistake executed a deed for the whole tract. Subsequently the defendant bought another piece within the tract deeded, thereby proving the original agreement. The court practically reformed the contract by compelling a reconveyance of the parts to which the defendant was not entitled.

These cases of reformation are brought by some writers under a special category of mistakes "in expression." The objection to such a phrase is that any variation between the will and the declaration of a single party may be regarded as a mistake in expression. The especial characteristic of these cases in which the contract is reformed is the existence of a real agreement between the parties which is independent of the written instrument.

In none of the foregoing cases in equity can there be said to be anything which would tend to disprove the main proposition, that a mistake as to the content of the act is immaterial. On the contrary, that proposition is rather confirmed. In each instance the defendant is compelled to show some equity whose protection can be secured without impairing any principle of the substantive law. The best proof of this is to be found in that class of cases in which relief is refused, whenever it would appear to be subversive of the principle set forth in Smith *v.* Hughes.

CHAPTER V

Mistake as to Fundamental Quality

According to Savigny, a mistake *in substantia* must be treated precisely like a mistake *in corpore* whenever, according to the views commonly prevalent in daily intercourse, the object belongs to a different category from that to which it was erroneously supposed to belong. This is the accepted German doctrine,[1] although there is at the same time a very respectable body of opinion to the effect that such a mistake is in reality a mistake in motive.

The Roman law rule of implied warranty of quality in sales is not rendered superfluous by Savigny's doctrine. Savigny himself admitted that mistakes in quality would not render acts void, unless such mistakes could be brought within his rule of the distinct category. The vendee who was mistaken in the quality of the article bought, and whose mistake did not amount to a mistake *in substantia*, could obtain relief only under one of the aedilitic remedies. The contract would be merely voidable.

In marked contrast to the Roman rule of warranty against hidden defects—a rule which may well be described as that of *caveat venditor*—is the common-law doctrine of *caveat emptor*. The common law in this respect is the exact reverse of the Roman law. The Roman doctrine is a direct help to a mistaken vendee. The common-law doctrine stands directly in the way of a vendee who desired to plead his mistake. It is applied indiscriminately to all sales and deliveries of chattels. No distinction is commonly drawn

[1] *Bürgerliches Gesetzbuch*, Sec. 119.

between mistakes in quality and mistakes *in substantia.* Consequently the rule of *caveat emptor* has impeded proper consideration of *error in substantia.*

Thus, in the early case of Chandelor *v.* Lopus,[1] known as the bezar-stone case, the court was asked to decide as to the effect of a mistake *in substantia.* A bezar stone is a calcareous growth in the stomach of certain ruminants, and was supposed to be a sure antidote for poison. The purchaser got some other kind of a stone. The sale was held valid.

In Beniger *v.* Corwin [2] it appeared that the plaintiff had exchanged his horse for the defendant's horse and note. The defendant believed that the plaintiff's horse was sound. The plaintiff knew his horse to be unsound. The court held that the defendant took the risk, and that the rule of *caveat emptor* applied, there being no duty to disclose defects.

In Street *v.* Blay,[3] the defendant bought a horse which turned out to be unsound. It was held that he must pay for it, and that his only relief was dependant upon the existence of a warranty.

In a similar case, Wheat *v.* Cross,[4] the defendant bought a horse, which turned out to be farcy. The court held that a mistake in the quality of the article purchased is of no effect. In the absence of a warranty, the rule of *caveat emptor* applies, and the buyer takes the risk of quality upon himself.

In Bryant *v.* Pember,[5] the defendant bought a cow which turned out to be worthless. The court held that in the absence of fraud or a warranty, the defendant was bound to pay for his purchase. The chattel "is at the risk of the buyer as to defects and unsoundness."

[1] Cro. Jac., 4. [2] 24 N. J. L., 257. [3] 2 B. & Ad., 456.
[4] 31 Md., 99. [5] 45 Vt., 487.

In Hecht *v.* Batcheller,[1] the plaintiff bought a note from a broker. It appeared that a short time before the sale the maker had failed. The court held that as there was no fraud and both parties were on an equal footing, and as no warranty could be implied, the sale must be treated as valid, the subject-matter itself being certain.

Cases of the preceding kind are innumerable in the common law. They are cited merely to illustrate the range of cases in which the rule of *caveat emptor* has been treated as decisive.

The rule has been stretched too far. If properly applied, it is not inconsistent with Savigny's doctrine of mistake *in substantia.* Of the cases cited above, only the bezar-stone case was wrongly decided. Under Savigny's doctrine such a mistake as was proved in that case would be regarded as a mistake *in substantia*, and would be treated as equivalent to a mistake *in corpore.*

Where the rule of *caveat emptor* does not stand in the way, the courts have treated mistake as to substance or fundamental quality in precisely the same manner in which they treat mistake as to the identity of the thing. In Harvey *v.* Harris [2] and Huthmacher *v.* Harris's Administrators,[3] already cited in the chapter on "Mistake in the Act," there was agreement *in corpore* and mistake as to the substance. *Caveat emptor* could not be invoked because the purchasers were not impugning the sales. In each case they were obtaining goods of greater value than they expected. The sales were attacked by the vendors, and were held to be void.

In recent cases in which the rule of *caveat emptor* was invoked the courts have shown a tendency to exclude its application when the mistake regarded the substance of the

[1] 147 Mass., 335.

[2] 112 Mass., 32; *supra*, p. 103.

[3] 38 Pa. St., 491; *supra*, p. 104.

thing sold. In such cases, however, the sale has not been treated as void but as merely voidable.

A notable exception to the rule of *caveat emptor* is to be found in the case of Griggsby *v.* Stapleton.[1] The defendant sold cattle which were afflicted with Texas fever. The plaintiff sued for the purchase price and recovered. The court held that "this defect affected the object for which they were to be used, the disease not being easily detected by the inexperienced." The case cannot be treated as a mistake *in substantia,* and must therefore be regarded as an exception to the rule of *caveat emptor.* In this respect it is unsupported.

Thwing *v.* Hall[2] is an instance of mistake *in substantia.* The plaintiff sold to the defendant what both parties at the time honestly thought was some virgin-forest land. In fact, it was already entirely denuded. The plaintiff brought action for specific performance; the defendant asked that the contract be canceled because of the mistake. The contract was canceled.

In Gompertz *v.* Bartlett,[3] the plaintiff bought what was supposed to be a foreign bill of exchange, which did not need a stamp. In fact, it was drawn in London, and was therefore unenforceable for want of such a stamp. The court held that the plaintiff could recover the purchase price.

The plaintiff in Jones *v.* Ryde[4] bought a navy bill which turned out to have been forged. There was no fraud on the part of the vendor. The plaintiff was allowed to recover on the ground that the difference in the object was so great as to constitute a failure of consideration.

It appeared in Irwin *v.* Wilson[5] that the plaintiff and defendant had exchanged their lands. The plaintiff owned

[1] 94 Mo., 423. [2] 40 Minn., 184. [3] 2 E. & B., 849.
[4] 5 Taunt, 488. [5] 45 Ohio St., 426.

some excellent land in Ohio, while the defendant owned some land in Iowa, which was supposed to be good land worth at least $10 per acre, but which was in fact very poor, wet land hardly worth $3 per acre. Neither party knew the actual condition of the Iowa land, but relied upon the statements of a third party, who thought he had inspected the land but had confused it with another tract. The court found no negligence and no fraud. The contract was rescinded.

Wood *v.* Boynton [1] is the well-known diamond case of Wisconsin. The plaintiff found a stone about the size of a pigeon's egg. She sold it to a jeweler, who bought it for one dollar as a specimen. Neither party knew its real character at the time. It turned out to be a diamond. The plaintiff, as it appeared, simply offered to sell it as a stone, without making any further inquiry, and the jeweler on his part simply offered to buy it as such. The court held that there was no "mistake made by the vendor in delivering an article which was not the article sold." There was no "mistake in fact as to the identity of the thing sold with the thing delivered upon the sale." Where there is such a mistake, "the thing delivered is not the thing sold, and no title passes to the vendee by such delivery." This case was correctly decided, because, as the court said, there was no mistake, or, as Savigny would say, no divergence between the will and declaration of either party. The case is in point because of its clear recognition, *obiter*, of a mistake *in substantia* in the common law.

In Sherwood *v.* Walker,[2] the defendant, who was a stock-breeder, sold to the plaintiff a cow which had been very valuable for breeding purposes but was believed to have become barren. Before delivery the defendant discovered that

[1] 64 Wis., 265.

[2] 66 Mich., 568.

the cow was with calf. He at once repudiated the contract and refused to deliver. The plaintiff insisted upon delivery being made, claiming that the cow was his, notwithstanding defendant's mistake. The court said that "the mistake was not of the mere quality of the animal. A barren cow is substantially a different thing than a breeding one." The animal in question was not

the kind of animal the defendant intended to sell, or the plaintiff to buy. She was not a barren cow, and if this fact had been known there would have been no contract. The mistake affected the substance of the whole consideration, and it must be considered that there was no contract to sell or sale of the cow as she actually was. The thing sold and bought had in fact no existence. She was sold as a beef creature would be sold; she is in fact a breeding cow and a valuable one.

This case clearly supports the proposition that a mistake *in substantia* is equivalent to a mistake *in corpore.*

The principle which should be applied in dealing with mistakes of this class is well stated in the English case of Kennedy *v.* Panama Company.[1] In this case it appeared that the West Indian Mail Company operated a line of ships from Southampton to Panama. The defendant company, which operated a line of ships from New Zealand to Panama, had issued a prospectus stating that it had concluded a contract with the New Zealand government to carry the English mails, connecting with the West Indian Mail Company at Panama. In order to carry into effect the provisions of the contract, it needed additional capital, and for this purpose it invited subscriptions to stock. The plaintiff, on the strength of this prospectus, subscribed for a certain number of shares. The New Zealand government repudi-

[1] L. R., 2 Q. B., 580.

ated its contract. The plaintiff sought to return his shares and to rescind his contract. The court found no fraud, and only an innocent misrepresentation. Blackburn, J., delivering the opinion of the court, said:

It was contended . . . that the effect of the prospectus was to warrant to the intended shareholders that there really was such a contract as is there represented, and not merely to represent that the company *bona fide* believed it; and that the difference between shares in a company with such a contract and shares in a company whose supposed contract was not binding, was a difference in substance, in the nature of the thing; and that the shareholder was entitled to return the shares as soon as he discovered this, quite independently of fraud, on the ground that he applied for one thing and got another. And, if the invalidity of the contract really made the shares he obtained different things in substance from those which he applied for, this would, we think, be good law. The case would then resemble Gompertz *v.* Bartlett [1] and Gurney *v.* Wormersley [2] . . . But where there has been an innocent misrepresentation, or misapprehension, it does not authorize a rescission unless it is such as to show that there was a complete difference in substance between what was supposed to be and what was taken, so as to constitute a failure of consideration.

The court cited the familiar passages from the Digest of Justinian to illustrate the distinction, and stated that the mistake, in the present instance, did not affect "the substance of the matter, for the applicant actually got shares in the very company in which he applied."

In view of the above decisions and dicta, there can be no question that there is a tendency in the common law to restrict the application of the rule of *caveat emptor* and to recognize the doctrine of *error in substantia*. It is clear,

[1] 2 E. and B., 849.

[2] 4 E. and B., 133.

moreover, that Savigny's criterion is being applied in order to distinguish *error in substantia* from mere mistake as to quality, the question being in each case whether the thing as it is falls in a different category from that to which it was mistakenly assigned. With the recognition of mistake in the substance, it is possible either to treat such a mistake as equivalent to *error in corpore* and to pronounce the contract void, as Savigny did and as the new German code does, or to treat the mistake as a mistake in motive merely, in which case the contract may be pronounced voidable on some such special ground as failure of implied condition precedent or failure of consideration.

CONCLUSION

It was stated, in the Introduction, that the attitude of the law regarding mistake in contract is determined by the existence of conflicting equities. It is inequitable, on the one hand, that the person who has made a declaration only because of a mistake should be held to an obligation which he has not meant to assume. It is inequitable, on the other hand, that the person who is entitled to suppose, and who does suppose, that the declaration made to him corresponds to the declarant's intention, should suffer damage, without fault on his part, by reason of the failure of the contract.

According as one or the other point of view appeals more strongly to theoretical writers, they become more or less thorough-going adherents of the subjective or of the objective theory of the juristic act. A contract is defined by the one school as the meeting of minds; by the other as the correspondence of declarations. Both schools recognize, of course, that when the separate declarations do not correspond there is no contract; but when the separate declarations do correspond, but the declaration of one party is not in accordance with his intention, they approach the problem from opposite starting-points. Neither school, however, has the full courage of its convictions. The objective theory is consistently applied only in early law, in which no obligation can be created without words of form and in which the form always binds. The subjective theory, likewise, is never applied without limitations of an important character. Its most pronounced adherents invariably start with the presumption that a declaration means what it seems to mean, *i. e.*, that a declaration is to be taken in the sense in which a person of average intelligence would take it under the given circumstances, and with the further presumption that the intention corresponds to the declaration unless the contrary is proved. They recognize also that the invisible will can be proved only by its external manifestations in words or in silence, in acts or in omissions, and that the real intent which they invoke against the declaration is itself only a thing inferred from such indicia. They affirm only that when it can be proved by such indicia that the declaration was not willed at all, or was not meant in the sense in which it appeared to be meant, the declaration is then in principle null, and its nullity entails the nullity of the contract of which it is a component part.

When we turn from theory to laws and decisions, we find that every legal system attempts a compromise between the conflicting equities of the contracting parties. The Roman law emphasizes the necessity of will and its exclusion by mistake: *errantis nulla voluntas.* The English law affirms that a meeting of the minds is necessary for agreement and that a real assent is essential to obligation. Both systems, however, subject this rule to important exceptions, for the protection of those who take declarations at their face value. In neither system is it permissible that he who has made an apparently clear declaration should subsequently allege a mental reservation, or that a man who has intentionally employed ambiguous words calculated to mislead should insist on his own interpretation of such words; for neither system permits that a man draw advantage from his own wilful wrong. Neither system permits a man to plead that he did not intend his declaration, unless he himself is honestly mistaken. Whether at Roman law the mistake cannot be plead unless it be excusable is disputed. Savigny declares that if the mistake be such as to exclude any real will, it makes no difference whether it be excusable or not. Given the premises of the subjective theory, this conclusion is logically unassailable. The majority of commentators, however, bar the plea of mistake in the case of gross negligence, and many of them take the same position as regards ordinary negligence. The latter position is that of the English law. As between the declarant whose mistake was due to his own carelessness and the other party who did not and could not perceive the erroneous assumption on which the declarant was acting, the equities of the latter are obviously stronger.

The re-affirmation in the new German code of the subjective theory in its extreme form, the legislative provision that the mistake which excludes real assent justifies the avoidance of the contract without regard to the negligence of the declarant, has been rendered possible only by the adoption of another method of satisfying the claims of the innocent party who was entitled to take, and did take, the declaration in its obvious meaning. The new solution consists in recognizing that party's "negative interest" in the existence of a contract and in awarding him "negative damages" for its failure. The contract is not upheld, but the party who has suffered damage through his reliance upon the declaration receives compensation. He is to be put in as good a position as if he had never been led to believe that he had a contract. If it can be shown that he was entitled to no such belief, his claim for negative damages is, of course, defeated.

Another limitation upon the subjective theory, which is common to the Roman and to the English law, is that not every mistake avoids the contract. In Roman as in English law a distinction is drawn, which Savigny was the first accurately to formulate, between mistake which excludes will and mistake which produces will. The latter mistake, mistake in motive, is regularly immaterial in both systems.

Within the category of mistakes which exclude correspondence between will and declaration, the Roman and English law alike disregard all but really important or "essential" mistakes. In both systems the standard of essentiality is objective and is practically the same. Mistake as to the nature of the act and mistake as to the thing which forms the object of the act are regularly essential; mistake in the person with whom the contract is made may or may not be essential, according to the circumstances of the particular case. In close cases, the English law seems more inclined than the Roman to regard mistake in the person as essential. Mistake as to especially important characteristics of the person or as to the fundamental quality or "substance" of the thing, a mistake which is regarded as essential in Roman law, is coming to be so regarded in English law, although the development of the principle is still obstructed by the improper extension frequently given to the maxim of *caveat emptor.*

When a contracting party has willed his declaration but not its content, *i. e.*, when he has wholly failed to appreciate the nature and extent of the obligation which his declaration properly entails, legislatures and courts, as well as writers, find themselves on very debatable ground. The Roman law is as little inclined as is the English to declare an act void or even voidable because the declarant has not foreseen the consequences of his act; but when it can be fairly said that the declaration, although willed, wholly misrepresents the declarant's actual intention, the Roman law is more ready than is the English to avoid the act. The doctrine of estoppel, not wholly unrecognized in the Roman law, has attained a much more extensive development in the English law; and at common law a mistake as to the content of the act is regularly excluded from consideration. In equity, however, not only is specific performance refused in such cases, but if back of the mistaken expression there is a substantial agreement of both parties, the contract may be reformed; and if there is no such agreement, and the erroneous assumption on which the declaration was based was discernible by the other party, the contract may be rescinded.

In the new German code not only is mistake as to the content of the act assimilated to lack of intention to make the declaration, but the objective standard of essentiality is abandoned. The only question is whether, but for the mistake, the mistaken party would have made the declaration. Here again the equities of the party who relies on the declaration are protected by his claim for negative damages; but it can hardly be doubted that the adoption of the subjective standard will increase litigation and make the decision of actual cases more difficult. Ingenious counsel may easily occupy much of the time of the courts with discussions as to the probable operation of a given mind under hypothetical circumstances; and even if the other party is clearly entitled either to positive or to negative damages, it will often be found difficult to decide on which theory his damages are to be measured.

Where two great systems like the Roman and the English, each representing the conclusions of a legally minded people after centuries of civilized life, disagree in the treatment of a special problem, the modern legislator may well assume that the question is debatable. When, however, these two systems agree, the legislator who proposes a new rule needs strong arguments to prove that it is either necessary or desirable. He must be prepared to show either that the new rule is simply a more correct statement of the principle recognized in the older decisions, or that conditions have so changed that the original rule is no longer adequate. In the matter of mistake in contract, the latter hypothesis is excluded. The problem is practically the same in every fully developed civilization, for its essential factors are the characteristics of the human mind and the interests of commercial intercourse. It is precisely in such matters that comparative jurisprudence stands on the firmest basis and promises the least disputable results.